THE POWER OF A POSITIVE SELF-IMAGE

CLIFFORD G. BAIRD, Ph.D.

This book is designed for your personal reading enjoyment and profit and also for group study. A leader's guide with Victor Multiuse Transparency Masters is available from your local Christian bookstore or from the publisher.

VICTOR BOOKS a division of SP Publications, Inc.

WHEATON, ILLINOIS 60187

Offices also in
Whitby, Ontario, Canada
Amersham-on-the-Hill, Bucks, England

Fourth printing, 1986

Most of the Bible quotations in this book are from the *New American Standard Bible,* © the Lockman Foundation 1960, 1962, 1963, 1968, 1971, 1972, 1973, 1975, 1977. Other Bible versions used include the *King James Version* (KJV); *The New Testament in Modern English* (PH), Revised Edition, © J.B. Phillips, 1958, 1960, 1972, permission of Macmillan Publishing Co. and Collins Publishers; *The Modern Language Bible: The Berkeley Version in Modern English* (BERK), © 1945, 1959, 1969, by Zondervan Publishing House. Used by permission; and *The Living Bible* (TLB), © 1971 by Tyndale House Publishers, Wheaton, Ill. Used by permission.

Recommended Dewey Decimal Classification: 158.1
   Suggested Subject Headings: PERSONAL DEVELOPMENT, SUCCESSFUL LIVING

Library of Congress Catalog Card Number: 82-62439
ISBN: 0-88207-316-8

© 1983 by SP Publications, Inc. All rights reserved
Printed in the United States of America

VICTOR BOOKS
A division of SP Publications, Inc.
      Wheaton, IL 60187

Contents

To my dear wife Donna,
my best friend,
and to our precious children,
Pauleen, Paul, Brent, Brenda, and Bradley,
whom we love dearly

Your Life Can Shine
Foreword

We read in the first book of the Bible, Genesis, "And God made two great lights, the greater light to rule the day, and the lesser light to rule the night; He made the stars also. And God placed them in the expanse of the heavens to give light on the earth" (vv. 16-17).

So we are told that the sun and the moon were created on the fourth day of Creation. Ever since then, these two great lights have been fulfilling God's purpose. The sun, the source of our light, is for our day; the moon, a reflection of that light, is for our night. Day and night they have provided the light for our physical world.

On the flight of *Apollo 15,* we were able to study these two lights. The sun was usually possible to see unless blocked by the earth or the moon. It was intensely bright. We saw the pure light of our sun undiminished or reduced by the atmosphere of earth. We spent three days exploring the lifeless surface of the moon. We returned with a personal knowledge of the power of these two lights.

Shortly after God placed the sun and the moon in the heavens, we are told that He decided to create man "in His own image" (Gen. 1:26). As you know, it wasn't long before the image became tarnished as man sinned and a spiritual darkness settled upon the face of the earth. Man was lost. He could no longer live his life to its fullest in harmony with God's image.

Then God, because of His great love for the people of the earth, decided to send a new light into the world. This one would bring light into our spiritual darkness. He sent His only Son, Jesus Christ. Jesus said, "I am the light of the world; he who follows Me shall not walk in the darkness, but shall have the light of life" (John 8:12). He came that we might have life and have it more abundantly. He came so we might again live "in His image."

When I traveled into space I sensed the mighty power of God. I felt His control over our spacecraft and I felt His presence and guidance while we were on the moon. He answered my prayer when I was confronted by a pressing technical problem. He seemed to guide us to the discovery of the white "Genesis" rock. I returned to the earth with a new awareness of God's power and His love. I believe I have been given a glimpse of what God intends for each of our lives. Now I believe I know how Adam and Eve must have felt when they were the only two humans on the earth and they enjoyed communication with God. I rededicated my life to the Lord.

My self-image was greatly enhanced after my flight because I felt God had touched me. Chances are that you will never travel where I have been, but you can also feel His touch. You can experience that personal relationship with the Lord by simply inviting Him to be your Lord and Saviour.

I realize there are so many forces trying to destroy us as individuals, as families, and as a country. We have great spiritual darkness upon the earth. More than ever we need to see God so we might live "in His image." We need teachers who would reveal God's plan.

Dr. Clifford Baird is one of these teachers. He is a very special teacher. Our ancestors came from the same part of Ireland. He has spent most of his life in service for the Lord. I am grateful that I could be used to introduce him and his book to you. I think you will be blessed by the exciting material on a positive, Bible-based self-image. You will clearly see how you can be a reflection of Jesus Christ and truly live your life "in His image." Your life can shine as a pure reflection of God Himself so that you are "the light of the world."

Col. James B. Irwin
President, High Flight Foundation
Colorado Springs, Colorado

1

What Is Self-Image?

"For as he thinks within himself, so is he" (Proverbs 23:7).

Our older daughter, Pauleen, sat staring down at the dining room table. A few moments later tears began to roll down her cheeks. Our younger daughter, Brenda, who is what we call our sympathetic crier, joined the emotional moment. I could see that our three sons, Paul, Brent, and Bradley, were also troubled.

This situation developed one night after supper while we were still at the table. We have always been a loving family, and that night the kids were having fun sharing many memories of their growing-up years. They were reminding each other of events that had taken place when they were little children back in Ontario, Canada. As in any family, there were those private, inside stories which generated great embarrassment for one and thunderous laughter for the rest. Well, such were our goings-on that night.

During that period of my life I had been wrestling with many thoughts about the individual differences of people. For I was becoming more preoccupied with some of the obvious behavior patterns of young people, especially as I observed the differences between the dominant and submissive types. I was asking questions such as:

- Why does one person succeed and another fail?
- Why does one adult assert himself in a situation while another passively accepts it?
- Why does one child emerge as the leader of the group while the others patiently wait for direction?

As a result of these and other introspective questions, I began to search for practical answers. The people I counseled led me to specific moments and critical incidents in their lives. We all can clearly recall events which were significant in forming who we perceive ourselves to be. In our memories these events are polarized, so that we remember extremely happy, positive times and also moments of severe pain and negative put-downs.

There are two major factors which determine how long these effects last in memory and how much they affect our image-development. The first factor is how significant the persons involved in the incident are to us. The more important their role in our lives, the more value we place on their behavior toward us. The second factor is a combination of the frequency and the intensity of repeated behavior. In other words, if a certain incident is repeated many times, the message will be imprinted more permanently. The emotional intensity with which it is communicated makes the content more believable and hence more permanent. Let me illustrate by returning to our family supper table.

I wanted to get into a serious discussion with my children dealing with critical incidents in their young lives, to see what effect these incidents had had upon them. To introduce the topic, I shared with them a story which took place about 30 years before, when I was a boy growing up in Belfast, Northern Ireland. I have two older brothers who are both very special to me and who played a vital role in my growing-up years. Trevor, the oldest, is now a pastor of a large Baptist church near Toronto. Neville is president of a management consulting firm in Wheaton, Illinois. The story I related to the kids that night had to do with something Neville doesn't even remember. Even that fact is important since I remember it as if it happened this morning.

We lived in a narrow, three-story tenement home in North Belfast. The only relief from winter cold was in the warmth from the fireplace in the kitchen. Evenings after we had our baths, we'd dash down the narrow staircase and into the kitchen, where we lined up in front of the fire. As I warmed up, I would jump up and down, developing a certain rhythm, and would sing at the top of my lungs. One evening after such an episode, Neville took me aside and went to great lengths to tell me what a horrible singer I was. I was nine years old at the time. Neville was five years older and my hero. I wanted to do everything with him and be just like him. I remember feeling not anger but humiliation. Even as I write this, I can recall the intense embarrassment I felt. A few weeks later, a group came to our home for a sing-along. I can still see myself sitting quietly, looking across the room at Neville for some approval to sing. It didn't happen.

To this very day, I am reluctant to sing out loud in my church. Sounds silly, doesn't it?

After I shared this story with my children, I asked them to think of moments in their lives which have caused them either to modify their behavior or reevaluate their own opinions of themselves. I was searching for incidents in our family that needed to surface so that we could deal with them.

As I watched Pauleen's tears, I wondered what could have troubled her. She was beautiful, lovable, personable—what could it have been? Finally she related a seemingly small incident which has had a profound effect on her life. It happened when she was in the fourth grade, back when she had double ponytails, a big smile, shining blue eyes, and socks pulled up neat and tight. She was prim and proper, and very responsible. One day as she was getting on the school bus for the ride home, she heard the driver ask, "Who is that homely child?" Pauleen was stunned. She was hurt. She felt embarrassed. She was quiet for the entire ride home. She now shared with us how she had reasoned out that parents are supposed to say their little girls are beautiful. But the driver must be telling the truth. So for all those years that careless, insensitive comment by a bus driver played havoc with her self-image and stole many happy moments from her life. Is it any wonder that Jesus said, "Every careless word that men shall speak, they shall render account for it in the day of judgment"? (Matthew 12:36)

Your Picture of You

Your self-image is the concept or picture you have of yourself. It is the way you think of yourself. Your self-image began to form early in life. In infancy you learned what was you and what was not you. You learned to respond to your name and acquire a sense of your own identity.

As you grew you developed an increasingly complex image of who you were. Your self-image was heavily influenced by Significant Others. These Significant Others in your childhood were probably parents, grandparents, siblings, and other family members. In the postpuberty period of early and late adolescence, the Significant Others came to include and often be dominated by friends, hero-type personalities, teachers, and other influences outside the basic family unit.

In your adult life, the Significant Others are employers, ministers, and influential friends or acquaintances, as well as family. Your self-image, therefore, is the compilation of feelings conveyed directly or indirectly by these Significant Others. In your interaction with them, you have come to see yourself very much as others see you. From their reactions, you learn what your qualities are and also the value of these qualities. You learn the things you do well and the things you do poorly. You learn how competent, acceptable, attractive, or lovable you are.

I believe that all your behavior—everything you do, everything you attempt, everything you say, everything you dream, everything you like, everything you dislike, everything—is subordinate to your self-image. When this self-image is formed, it becomes resistant to change. Self-image is not permanent; it can be changed, but there is a definite resistance. If you believe you can't do something, you avoid it or do it badly and so prove to yourself what you believe. Believing you can do something, you give it a good try and prove you can. In brief, you tend to validate your beliefs about yourself. What you do every day is a product of how you see yourself and also of the situation you are in. While your situation may change from day to day or from place to place, the things you believe about yourself are always present factors in determining your behavior.

The socialization process of any culture is a passing down, from one generation to the next, of value systems composed of mores and folkways. Each culture places a worth or value on behaviors. Certain behaviors and accomplishments are given higher values and therefore become standards of excellence. These standards are the goals and objectives with which the culture attempts to influence the lives of its people. They are the measuring sticks of success or failure.

In our society it so happens that we position ourselves and others most often by wealth, education, heritage, and possessions. It is not the way designed by God, but man's craving nature always emerges. This nature was first evidenced in the Garden of Eden when Eve did not resist her drive to be like God. This desire to be like her Creator resulted from her passion to be number one. She could not stand the thought of being a servant but wanted the position and the influence she felt she deserved. Immediately after Eve succumbed, she applied the most basic pressure known to man—peer pressure. Let us not self-righteously condemn Adam and Eve, for we are all social beings. And we all react to peer pressure. We are all victimized by the desire to be loved and accepted by others.

Development of Self-Image
The critical period for establishing a strong and healthy self-image is in the early years of development. Little children are

vulnerable to the behavior of parents and other family members. A young couple told me a sad story that still makes them feel guilty and angry. They have four children, two boys and two girls. Their second child is a girl who very early gave evidence that she would be a bed wetter. She seemed to have no control. Her parents tried everything but she did not respond. Her problem was not confined to bedtime—she would often be found wet during the day.

Finally in desperation, her parents took her to their family physician for a complete examination. X rays were taken and a diagnosis given. The doctor did not view the X rays himself but relied on expert opinion and evaluation. He concluded that there was no physiological problem, that the little girl was lazy and needed consistent discipline. These loving parents felt strongly that discipline, if given in love, was in fact an act of love. As time wore on, the little girl still did not respond. If anything, she got worse, and began to tell powerfully believable stories to explain to her parents why she was wet. Unfortunately, these stories were all lies. But she too was under great pressure and tension as she was being punished for something she could not control.

Several years later the parents ordered more X rays and discovered that her problem was physiological, not psychological. It was treated surgically, but her emotional scars remain. Through those very formative years she was imprinted with feelings of low self-worth. Her parents did not mean this to happen, and are agonizing over the results. Because of negative, crushing moments, the girl needs a great overdose of tenderness and love to overcome the past and reshape her life for the future. Her self-image can and will change, but it will take a definite concerted effort of all the Significant Others in her life.

The Bible tells us clearly there is only one quality that never fails. In his beautiful love chapter, 1 Corinthians 13, the Apostle Paul tells us: "Love never fails" (v. 8). Isn't that wonderful? And he explains what love is.

Love endures long and is kind; love is not jealous; love

is not out for display; it is not conceited or unmannerly; it is neither self-seeking nor irritable, nor does it take account of a wrong that is suffered. It takes no pleasure in injustice but it sides happily with truth. It bears everything in silence, has unquenchable faith, hopes under all circumstances, endures without limit (1 Corinthians 13:4-7, BERK).

The Reinforcement Principle

In graduate school I took a course in experimental psychology. While I didn't really enjoy the course, one thing happened in it that changed my life. We saw an old black and white movie which began with two pigeons playing Ping-Pong. You can imagine how a scene like that livens up an 8 o'clock class. As we sat glued to this choreography, we saw the ball roll into the net and one of the pigeons drop the bat from its mouth and hop over to the scoreboard. As it pecked the right spot, the score flashed 20—20. Now if you play Ping-Pong, you know that when the score is 20—20, you must win by two points. Well, the pigeons knew this too.

After the game, the film flashed back to a Ping-Pong table without a net, and with a paddle lying at one end of the table. Then it showed the pigeon entering for the first time and being placed at the opposite end of the table from the paddle. The long-range objective of the experiment was to teach the pigeon to play Ping-Pong. But that could not be accomplished at one sitting. Therefore, short-range goals were developed. The experiment was conducted under two generally accepted laws of learning.

● Behaviors which are reinforced are most likely to recur.

● People and animals will learn only what they have to in order to accomplish their goals.

The reinforcement principle plays a very important role in learning. The initial short-run objective was to have the pigeon pick up the paddle. But to accomplish this the pigeon had to learn to face the right direction after being placed on the table. The experimenter observed every movement of the pigeon closely. Each time the pigeon would turn even slightly in the right direction, he would give it a food reward. It wasn't long until that pigeon realized that there was a "right" way to face and a "wrong" way to face. When the experimenter would bring it out for another conditioning session and would face it the wrong way, the pigeon would actually hurry to get turned the right way. The pigeon was gradually conditioned to walk up the table in the direction of the paddle, then to pick up the paddle, then to hit the ball, and on and on, until the pigeon was able to play and score a complete game of Ping-Pong. The same conditioning was done with two other pigeons. The conditioning was so thorough that the pigeons knew that they only served the ball five times. On one occasion when the experimenter tossed the ball a sixth time, the pigeon recognized this to be one too many serves and let the ball roll off the table.

Reinforcement by Love

Everything in God's creation responds to the two basic emotions of love and fear. Both of these are major motivational forces in our lives. Obviously the pigeons had no idea they could play Ping-Pong, but the experimenter did. He knew that love never fails, and that reinforcement always works. If this principle works so effectively with animals, you can imagine what can be accomplished in human beings. This is why the Apostle Paul spent so much time encouraging the early believers in the New Testament churches. He taught them and shared with them; he admonished them and loved them.

To the church at Philippi, Paul wrote: "I can do all things, through Him who strengthens me" (Philippians 4:13), or "I have strength for every situation through Him who empowers me" (BERK). Too many Christians are unaware of their position in Christ. Too many believers are leading anemic lives, falling victim to the enemy of our souls. In response to the question, "What is the chief end of man?" the *Westminster Catechism* replies, "To glorify God and enjoy Him forever." How can we glorify God if we do not recognize that

He is greater than the prince of this world? I believe the greatest victory Satan achieves is the quenching of the full potential God intends for His children.

The secret to accomplishment lies in our willingness to attempt new things. You likely have heard the saying, "It is better to shoot at something and miss than to shoot at nothing and hit." A major reason the world has never been evangelized is that too many Christians do not really believe it can be done.

Henry Ford once said, "Think you can or think you can't, either way you will be right." Why is that? Because we work to validate our perceptions. The process of proving our assumptions correct is called self-fulfilling prophecy. We actually cause an event to occur. Imagine what could be accomplished if we really believed we could evangelize the world. It would be done. But this is where Satan disarms God's people by urging them toward feelings of inferiority.

The only way to overcome these feelings is by love. Parents need to love each other more. Parents need to love their children more demonstratively. Children should love parents and siblings more. We must show our love and concern for each other. There is no power anywhere which can conquer love. Love is the act of encouraging a person who is attempting something new. Love is creating a dream for someone to live by. Love is caring enough for each other that we actually promote one another's concerns, putting them before our own.

Personal Freedom

A strong and healthy self-image which is in accord with God's Word will lead to personal freedom. Have you ever wondered about the word *freedom?* What does it bring to mind? When I think of freedom I hear children laughing. I hear church bells ringing. I see Old Glory blowing in the wind. And I think of eagles soaring. The eagle is the only bird that flies so high it actually loses sight of earth. That reminds me of the words of a hymn, "And the things of earth will grow strangely dim, in the light of His glory and grace."

Many people are imprisoned within low self-image. They will never attempt much because they don't see themselves as able to accomplish much. Freedom means not being in bondage. I know people who need to be set free from despair to experience joy, from their problems to tranquillity, from loneliness to fullness of life, from rejection to acceptance, from inferiority to self-confidence. Others need to be freed from the past to be able to enjoy the present. They are so accustomed to failure that they expect it.

In Deuteronomy 6 we read God's plan for parents as they teach their children. I am confident this plan is transferable to every situation of life. This plan presents a methodology for teaching important principles:

> And these words, which I am commanding you today, shall be on your heart; and you shall teach them diligently to your sons and shall talk of them when you sit in your house and when you walk by the way and when you lie down and when you rise up.
>
> And you shall bind them as a sign on your hand and they shall be as frontals on your forehead. And you shall write them on the doorposts of your house, and on your gates (6:6-9).

If you want your children to grow up well taught in godly principles of life, spend time with them. This directive from God is truly a saturation approach. Every possible opportunity for training is covered. In writing to the Philippian church, the Apostle Paul said that they were to think on things that were true, honest, just, pure, lovely, and of good report (4:8). In other words, don't allow your mind to be filled with that which will corrupt it. Don't saturate your thoughts with negative debris that will affect your perception of life. For your thoughts determine your actions. And your actions determine your accomplishments.

Paganini was a great violinist who held his audiences enraptured, as they waited for each new thrust of the bow on his magnificent Stradivarius.

One day as Paganini was about to come on stage, he reached to pick up his violin and saw that the instrument was not his Stradivarius but an old, beaten-up violin. He rushed about frantically searching, but couldn't find it. Finally he concluded that someone had stolen it.

He peered out between the curtains and saw that the opera house was full. He felt almost nauseous as he thought about the evening performance, and nearly talked himself into not going on stage. And yet he realized this was an opportunity to show people that music is not in the instrument but in the soul of the artist.

So Paganini took a deep breath and walked out to a great ovation. He captured the audience immediately by sharing with them his dilemma. Then he went on to play as he had never played before. The crowd went wild with applause. For in that brief moment of life, they saw a greatness that would not be encumbered by circumstances, that chose to summon up what was already there. It took a crisis for Paganini to prove that the music was not in the instrument but indeed in the soul.

Self-Perpetuation

What then is the commodity we call self-image? It appears that each individual collects and organizes thousands of pieces of information about himself that vary in clarity, precision, and importance. Self-image should be understood not as a thing but as an organization of ideas.

Self-image is self-perpetuating. It has a circular effect, for it corroborates already existing beliefs about self, and so tends to reinforce and maintain its own existence. This circular characteristic of the self-image is often seen in the problems children have with arithmetic, spelling, public speaking, physical education, or other school subjects. It now seems clear that many children do poorly in certain subjects because they believe they cannot achieve.

The self-perpetuating effect of the self-image is by no

means limited to success or failure in academic subjects. This same dynamic may be seen at work in all aspects of life. Fortunately, the circular effect operates equally well in positive directions. People who believe they can are more likely to succeed.

As I read the first chapter of the Book of Joshua, I am impressed by the fact that three times God told Joshua to be strong and courageous. "Have not I commanded you? Be strong and courageous! Do not tremble or be dismayed, for the Lord your God is with you wherever you go" (v. 9; see also vv. 6-7). These motivating and encouraging words from the Lord were paving a path for Joshua to follow. God instilled him with confidence and assurance that God plus one is a majority.

Joshua accepted and believed that he could achieve with God's help. "Then Joshua commanded the officers of the people, saying, 'Pass through the midst of the camp and command the people saying, "Prepare provisions for yourselves, for within three days you are to cross this Jordan, to go in to possess the land which the Lord your God is giving you, to possess it"'" (vv. 10-11).

Everything we do in life is subordinate to our self-image. Once formed, it resists change but is not permanently set. Therefore it is essential that we instill in each other those personal affirmations which will cause us to dream dreams and to face life's circumstances in the reality of doing all things through Christ.

"Think you can or think you can't, either way you will be right."

2

Negative Self-Image

"Men do not see the light which is bright in the skies" (Job 37:21).

Emotional nearsightedness is a condition which plagues those unable to look beyond the debris of the moment to see potential in every situation. This condition does not belong only to the weak. On the contrary, some of the greatest heroes of the Bible suffered from it. Judging by the depths to which they fell, a few were totally overwhelmed.

A little while ago Donna and I, and my brother Neville and his wife Peggy were privileged to spend some time with friends on the beautiful Fort Myers Beach in Florida. I was the guest speaker at a three-day seminar for Newton and Associates, a real estate firm.

One evening we were invited to supper as guests of Vern and Meryl Ericksson and Jim and Ellie Newton, the owners of the firm. As we centered our thoughts on the things of the Lord, we listened as Ellie Newton, a dear saint of 80 years, shared with us her love of her Saviour Jesus Christ. Her husband, Jim, told us how he met the Lord on his way to a dance—a serendipitous happening some would say, and yet it was truly a moment of destiny.

The intended purpose of our evening together was to discuss some of the more unusual happenings in their lives. Jim could have spent the evening telling us stories about his close friend, Thomas Edison. For many years Jim spent the winters with the Edisons in Fort Myers.

Should he have run out of Edison stories, Jim could have continued by telling about his friend, Henry Ford. It seems that Ford dearly loved Edison and as a result bought a home beside him in Fort Myers. Jim's relationship with Edison brought him in contact with Harvey Firestone, and for many years he was Firestone's chief assistant.

I asked Jim Newton what it was about him that these men liked the most. He replied by way of another story example. He had become a close friend of Dr. Alexis Karrel, the father of modern surgery. One day Dr. Karrel introduced him to Charles Lindbergh. About 30 minutes after their meeting, Dr. Karrel asked Jim, "Tell Charles about the night you were going to the dance and missed it." It is a humorous story of the events surrounding Jim's conversion, but it had a deep impact on these famous men. It was a building block for trust and confidence.

The relationship between Jim Newton and Charles Lindbergh grew to such a point of trust and friendship that Charles Lindbergh was the best man at Jim and Ellie's wedding. Their close friendship lasted for more than 40 years.

Sometimes I still find it hard to believe that we met one person who was acquainted with Charles Lindbergh, Thomas Edison, Henry Ford, Harvey Firestone, and Dr. Alexis Karrel. I am afraid if I were Jim Newton, I would feel that I was a somebody. But Jim considered it much more important to discuss his relationship with God through Jesus Christ His Son than to talk about his relationship with famous people. To me this was a tribute to his love for the Lord.

God was gracious to Jim Newton to surround him with men who would encourage him and, through example, show him how to see beyond the discouragement of any given situation. Life did not cease when these great inventors were frustrated by research and development that seemed to come to a dead end. They each had an eye focused on completing the goal at hand.

On one occasion when Mr. Edison went to his lab, he saw that his chief researcher was discouraged, and said, "Meadowcroft, we are making fantastic progress. We have found 1,000 ways it won't work." Edison, who patented 1,097 inventions, was 90 percent deaf. Yet many of Mr. Edison's inventions, such as the phonograph and office dictating machines, depended on being able to hear! After the terrible tragedy in the Lindbergh family, life did not end. In the heartbreaking times, we can go on and overcome by the grace of God.

One problem most of us face is that often our faith depends more on what God does than on who He is. He is sovereign and even though I cannot comprehend His work, I must be willing to act on His promises. I must determine to activate my will and like the psalmist be ready to say, "I will sing of the mercies of the Lord forever" (Psalm 89:1, KJV). Not everyone is as blessed as Jim and Ellie Newton to be so surrounded with encouragement. And lest I paint a picture with skies too blue and pastures too green, these dear saints of God have been called to walk where few have gone and to bear the burdens of many. They know the One in whom they have believed and are persuaded that He is able to keep them until they see Christ.

There are many who do not know their position in Christ and as a result do not give God the glory in every circumstance. We were not promised that all things would be good in and of themselves. But we were promised that they would turn out for our good, if we let them.

Depression

If self-image begins in infancy, grows with increasing complexity, and is influenced substantially by the Significant Others in our lives, then we should not be surprised to learn that millions of people have been robbed of their full potential by being given an unhealthy self-image. The curse of low self-image is poor, unstable performance in all areas of life. The curse is the fear to initiate, to attempt new things. The curse is to attempt new things, never to finish them. The curse is the experience, almost daily, of a sense of powerlessness and meaninglessness.

The curse follows a well-laid design that causes turmoil sufficient to frustrate every purpose and goal a person has. If this happens early in life, it can prevent the person from any real accomplishment. Ultimately, the curse leads one into a state of habitual depression.

Depression is self-perpetuating and is fed on the following foods:

● Frustration. A person feels frustrated when he has been prevented from accomplishing a purpose or desire. Or it may come when another person nullifies an accomplishment or makes an achievement appear insignificant or ineffective.

Not long ago I heard a radio interview with a missionary who spoke of the frustration he feels when stateside Christians tend to ridicule his emphasis on foreign missions. He told how discouraged he becomes when he is questioned on the ineffectiveness of mission endeavors. He wonders if he is wasting his life rather than giving it.

Satan is a wily foe who can effectively use the tongues of self-centered Christians to frustrate the work of any pastor, missionary, or Christian worker.

● Disillusionment. When a person is disillusioned, he becomes disenchanted and loses his sense of direction. While there is never an excuse for getting sidetracked and for backsliding from the Lord, yet there are situations for which certain people will have to answer one day, if they have caused others to stumble and become disillusioned with the things of the Lord.

I am reminded of a young boy who grew up on the mission field, the son of a "successful" missionary. He was not the most agreeable boy ever to go through the school for missionary children, but that was no excuse for the behavior of the Significant Others in his life. On repeated occasions he was told he was "possessed" and "incorrigible." He remembers that one particular dorm parent never showed him real love or true discipline. The boy never forgot this and became bitter and disillusioned. Today he is wandering a long way from God. While we know that he is ultimately responsible before God and will be held accountable for every unconfessed sin, it is also true that God will deal severely with those who caused such hurt and disillusionment.

● Discouragement. When a person is discouraged, he loses confidence. This hinders any effort to achieve, and he then feels dejected and without hope. This can be seen in the adult who spends his life constantly searching for fulfillment. It also explains the "occupational tourist," the person who hops from one job to the next and stays just long enough to take all the right "pictures" and then becomes bored and starts out for "new adventures."

How sad it is to come to mid-life and be faced with an array of short-term excursions but no accomplishments, because there has been no commitment.

I know a man who has spent all his life searching for fulfillment. His father abandoned the family when my friend was a teenager. He was oppressed by this rejection and attempted to restore a relationship with his dad. This became his life's mission, but on almost every occasion his desire was thwarted. His father had little real concern for him. As the oldest child and only son, he felt the burden and pressure of the family circumstances.

Throughout his life he was looking for someone or something to complete his life. But all too often he found those who competed rather than completed. As a result he rejected relationships with other men who desired to be surrogate fathers. He changed jobs and vocations several times, hoping each one would bring him the satisfaction he craved. His demands on himself became untenable as he sought for something he would never find. He looked for peace in objects and events. He assumed that tranquillity and satisfaction were to be found in some Shangrila free from any trial and tribulation.

What he was looking for was someone to love and encourage him, someone to reinforce his strengths and cover his weaknesses. After he struggled for 20 years, his search ended when he took himself off the throne of his life and allowed his Saviour to take absolute control. Only then did he find peace. Only then did he find tranquillity in the storm.

Nevertheless, the source of his discouragement had been very real. The lesson for all of us is that we never know the potential of the person we are influencing when we take time to encourage and build up. However, God knows, and we can be His instruments of mercy and love.

● Hostility and apathy. If frustration, disillusionment, and discouragement feed depression, then hostility and apathy are its offspring. Hostility and apathy are on opposite ends of a behavioral continuum and are the manifestations most often observed in one suffering from a low self-image.

Recent newspaper articles on the prevalence of vandalism in schools attribute it to the low self-image of certain student groups. Violence is a statement of hopelessness and meaninglessness. Apathy is a total lack of emotion or feeling. One who is apathetic displays no interest in things generally found exciting, interesting, or moving. Apathy is yet another statement of hopelessness or meaninglessness.

A Biblical Perspective
Most people who have suffered frustration, disillusionment, and discouragement have at some time asked, "Why, Lord?" or "Why me, Lord?" A study of Psalm 77 reveals the origins and characteristics of depression and the antidote for it.

We find the psalmist lamenting in ancient terms:

Will the Lord reject forever? And will He never be favorable again? Has His loving-kindness ceased forever? Has His promise come to an end forever? Has

God forgotten to be gracious? Or has He in anger withdrawn His compassion? (Psalm 77:7-9)

1. Four Origins of Depression

● We enjoy being sad. Psalm 77:2 says, "My soul refused to be comforted." This was an obvious act of the will. The psalmist was being offered comfort, but he enjoyed being sad and consciously refused to accept help. I have met my share of those who suffer from a martyr complex. They truly enjoy their problems and decline any help whatsoever.

● An offending conscience. Verse 3 commences, "When I remember God, then I am disturbed." Here the Spirit of God is causing a wandering child to remember. Certainly, if we willfully do nothing about such correction, we can try all we like, but we will not remove the spot. Our conscience is a gift from God and He uses it to call attention to sin. If we regard wickedness in our hearts, the Lord will not hear us (Psalm 66:18). He will not listen. If we remember God's correction but do nothing about it, we will become depressed.

● A complaining spirit. "When I sigh" (v. 3) can be translated "when I complain." The word here translated "sigh" is translated "complaint" in Psalm 55:2 and 142:2.

The word *complain* stands alone as a graphic illustration of how the Children of Israel grumbled, whined, whimpered, and muttered at how God was dealing with them. Complaining is a by-product of a negative attitude, but it also feeds it. The more complaining we do the more we find to do. The more we complain the more depressed we become.

● Too much introspection. In the second half of verse 6, the psalmist portrays the sinful side of self-esteem—trying to solve problems outside of God's way and by our own wisdom. We read, "I will meditate with my heart; and my spirit ponders." Here we have the classic picture of one diligently searching his own heart. How can we know our own hearts when God declares that our hearts are deceitful and desperately wicked? The more we search for solutions, and yet neglect God and His Word, the more we will come up emptyhanded. This will only tend to magnify our inabilities and deepen our feelings of depression.

2. Four Characteristics of Depression

● Overwhelmed. In Psalm 77:3 the psalmist shares a characteristic common to many who believe they have been abandoned by God because they cannot see their way out. We read, "My spirit grows faint." How many times have you said, "What's the use? This is too much for me. Where is God anyhow? He doesn't really care. He has forgotten all about me. His promises apply to everyone but me." Most of us at one time or another have felt like calling it quits.

Some time ago I was dealing with a young man who had come to the conclusion that the best thing for all concerned would be for him to end his life. He was overwhelmed with the thought of the future because he could not cope with the problems of insecurity, family upheaval, and financial pressure. He was a Christian but felt he had been deserted by God. He was like the disciples in the sudden storm on the Sea of Galilee. They were perplexed when the storm suddenly came; but they were more terrified when they concluded that Jesus didn't care. As fishermen, they had faced many storms. Their panic was the result of the ultimate fear that Jesus really didn't care for them or for their safety.

When we are overwhelmed, it is not because of the problems but because we have no one who cares. When we sense that we are facing life alone, terror strikes our hearts. In every situation we need to echo the words of our Saviour, "Lo, I am with you always, even to the end of the age" (Matthew 28:20).

● Robbed of sleep. How many times have worry and anxiety resulted in sleepless nights? In the stillness and solitude of the nighttime, we tend to dwell on what is uppermost in our minds. If we are unable to cope with the day-to-day struggles of life, and if we believe we are facing these events alone, depression will result in sleeplessness.

Look at the beginning of verse 4—"Thou hast held my

eyelids open." We are robbed of sleep when we fail to fill our minds with the precious things of our Lord. Night is the perfect time to meditate on His love and tender mercy. Unfortunately, the pressure of depression forces us into an emotional prison with no available means of escape, until we learn that depression is the consequence of not leaning on the faithful, everlasting arms of our Lord.

When we do not sleep, we throw our physiological metabolism into imbalance. Sleep activates a chemical process which flushes the brain and enables it to be revitalized for effective service the next day. Sleeplessness hinders this cleansing program which God established for our bodies. A lack of sleep magnifies every problem and concern. Since we are unable to think clearly, we are driven into a deeper cycle of fear and anxiety which only tends to heighten our inability to sleep. Satan then alerts his forces against us.

- Dumbfounded. In verse 4 we read, "I am so troubled that I cannot speak." Have you ever been dumbfounded? Totally speechless? When we are pleasantly surprised and thrilled, we sometimes cannot say anything. At a time like this, my Donna simply cries. For her most recent birthday, the women in the church had a surprise party for her at a local country club. My secretary arranged the whole affair and Donna never guessed a thing. I was told that when she saw all the ladies she was speechless, thrilled, and couldn't do anything but cry.

There is a similar behavioral reaction to anticipated danger or overwhelming deep-rooted fear. When our thoughts are consumed with problems and we perceive a situation to be hopeless, we become dumbfounded. Even when we try to speak, our voices crack and our mouths dry up. Fear is a very real emotion. Depression is a very real experience. A leading indicator of a person slipping into deep depression is his desire to be silent. Speechlessness is the result of the mind being too preoccupied on inner thoughts to consider verbalizing.

- Nostalgic. Not too long ago Donna and I were going

through some old family albums and looking at old family slides. We don't do it often, and that night I discovered why. Instead of causing us to feel happy, it left us depressed. The thought of the children being small and toddling around the house in diapers brought to the surface a certain sadness that is difficult to describe. Obviously we are not sad that they have grown up healthy or that they love the Lord and wish to serve Him. This is truly a blessing and a joy. There is, however, a lingering thought about all the special moments such as school plays, broken collar bones, musicals, piano lessons, sports events, runny noses, and doctor visits. The hard times of the "good old days" have long been obscured by a desire to return to those days once again, if only for a little while.

The psalmist declared, "I have considered the days of old, the years of long ago" (v. 5). This is a deadly potion if we are discontent or unfulfilled in our present relationships. One sure way to be dissatisfied with life is to dwell on things which are past and gone forever. If we feel that we are not able to enjoy life as we did before, we will be overwhelmed and depressed. The enemy of our souls will marshall all his forces to cause us to give up and do nothing for God.

I read a hypothetical letter sent from Lucifer to his demon forces worldwide. He was commissioning them to do all they could to cause missionaries to become depressed and quit. In the letter he was giving a high grade to one of his lieutenants who thought of a sure way to get missionaries to think of the "good old days." He said their research had discovered that at the going-away celebration in the local churches, missionaries should hear many people tell them, "We are really going to miss you." In fact, the evening should be filled with fun, food, and fellowship. The more this special evening dwells on how much they will be missed, the greater will be the loneliness they face on the mission field. During emotional stress, missionaries will be most vulnerable to the "good old days" attack and Satan will be able to knock them off track.

There is no doubt about it—yesteryear has always been a popular theme, for it seems as though the past was tranquil and fulfilling. A little sign which hangs in one of our offices says, "Today is the tomorrow you feared yesterday." Today will become a yesterday. Right now we must make the most of what God provides for us today.

3. The Antidote for Depression

We find that the psalmist gives us a four-part antidote for depression. Because this is God's program, the cure is assured. But it must be followed like any other formula if we want to be successful in overcoming the curse of a negative self-image—depression.

● Confession. We must accept personal responsibility for our actions. Scripture is filled with declarations of human wills being at enmity against God. It is not natural for man to confess his sin, admit his mistakes, or say "I'm sorry." But God has determined that confession must pave the way for renewal in our relationship with Him. "If we confess our sins, He is faithful and righteous to forgive us our sins and to cleanse us from all unrighteousness" (1 John 1:9).

Confession is an admission of our inability, a recognition of our imperfection, and a declaration of our need to be rightly related to Him. The act of confession is a sign of a penitent spirit and opens the heart for new growth and maturity.

The psalmist continues: "Then I said—'It is my grief'" (v. 10). He is confessing to God and showing us a model by saying, "This is my problem. This is a self-inflicted wound and I assume personal responsibility for it."

How good it is to hear folks say, "I'm sorry; I did it. It is my fault." It is especially a blessing when our children are willing to confess, even to each other, their faults, their attitudes, their lack of appreciation, or whatever it was that separated them. How much more God must be thrilled when His children are anxious to follow the model He has made plain in His Word. The first step in the antidote, then, is to confess our infirmities to God, to admit our faults, and assume full responsibility for them.

● Confirmation. The process of confirmation is the act of supporting a statement by evidence. It is insufficient to merely say, "I'm sorry," without supporting it with specific behavioral evidence. The psalmist took particular action, "I will remember the deeds of the Lord; surely, I will remember Thy wonders of old." Here we are faced with the reality of willfully focusing our minds on the things of the Lord and His past faithfulness to us.

Proverbs 22:28 warns, "Do not remove the ancient boundary which your fathers have set." The children of Israel had made it a habit as they journeyed in the Promised Land to build altars to God. These were the ancient landmarks. Any time the people began to wonder if God was really concerned about them, they could return to an altar and remember a specific occasion of God's faithfulness. In like manner, we should establish landmarks of faith and drive them like stakes into the ground so that our families, and especially our children, will remember the specific situations in which God was real. If we should ever doubt who God is, we will be able to return to the stake we drove into the ground and remember exactly how He met our needs.

"Never doubt in the dark what God told you in the light." It is easy for us to lose sight of God's plan for our lives when we are besieged from every side. God has not changed and we must continue to keep on keeping on, especially when things are bleakest. God will be faithful to us as He has always been.

● Communication. Once we have confessed and have confirmed by our behavior that we mean business with God, then we should discipline ourselves to stay in touch with Him. The psalmist outlines for us the pattern and content of our communication. "I will meditate on all Thy work, and muse on Thy deeds" (v. 12). We are to nurture ourselves on the Word of God. We are to study it and hide it in our hearts. We are to ponder on the things of God and to share them with others. If speechlessness is one of the characteristics of depression, then talking would be a very direct cure to the problem. Our speech is to be on the work and deeds of the Lord. The psalmist is really saying that if we spend our time considering what God has done for us and are willing to share our testimony with others, then we will have no time for idle introspection. Our lives will be more profitably spent in meditation and witnessing. Communication with God is a combination of reading His Word, meditating on it, praying, and witnessing. This kind of communication is an essential ingredient in the antidote for depression.

• Communion. In the *King James Version* verse 13 is rendered, "Thy way, O God, is in the sanctuary." With a little contextual license, I want to suggest that the final step in the antidote for depression is fellowship with other believers. Satan is anxious for God's children to remain divided and isolated.

Most of us have had times when we just didn't feel like going to church or attending prayer meeting and Bible study. It was duty and habit that made us go. But when we got there and the clouds lifted, joy entered into our souls and we were blessed abundantly.

The fellowship of the early church must have really been something special. They were facing excruciating trials and needed the support and love of other Christians. Times haven't changed a lot, needs are the same, and people still need fellowship. Our Lord graciously adorns us with His presence when only two or three are gathered together in His name.

Confession, Confirmation, Communication, and Communion—these are the antidote for depression which is the curse of a negative self-image.

3

Causes of a Negative Self-Image

"Watch over your heart with all diligence, for from it flow the springs of life" (Proverbs 4:23).

God created us for His pleasure and for His honor and glory. We were designed to walk uprightly and to accomplish our very best. Yet most of us have never been able to cut free from the bondage of self-doubt which results in a negative self-image. Let us examine the four major causes of a negative self-image.

Careless Comments by Significant People

Parents, family members, friends, teachers, leaders, employers who have been the most significant people in our lives are often the agents who have caused us to see ourselves negatively. They may not be aware of the damage their actions or comments have caused. Their barrage of inappropriate and insensitive comments may have been a reaction to some event in their own lives which caused them to lapse momentarily. Whatever precipitated those moments, they had a severe and lasting impact on our lives.

A few years ago, our youngest daughter, Brenda, came home from school one day with a troubled and depressed look. I could see that she was both worried and frustrated. Just before supper I called her to her bedroom and asked what was nagging at her. She began to cry and told me how her teacher had embarrassed her. As she shared the whole incident with me, I could see that the potential damage was a whole lot more than embarrassment.

One of her teachers asked Brenda and her girlfriend to come to his classroom after school. He began the conversation with them by telling Brenda that she was irresponsible. He based his accusation on the fact that she had left her girlfriend's school pictures on her desk when she left class. It turned out that the girls had simply miscommunicated. Brenda thought her friend had seen her leave them there. The teacher assumed much more than he should have and began to lecture Brenda on irresponsibility.

Teachers are special people to our family, and we respect and admire them. In our home we value discipline. When a child was in trouble at school, he was in trouble at home. However, this particular incident was too serious to simply let pass, for Brenda was anything but irresponsible. I spoke to the teacher the next day to clear up the issue of the pictures. But I spent more time sharing how easily young people are pushed off track and begin to be what they believe others see them to be.

Not long ago I heard a mother say to her son, "Billy, you are the clumsiest boy I have ever seen." The truth of the matter is that he was the clumsiest boy I had ever seen. But my question was—how did he get that way?

It might have happened by what is known as a self-fulfilling prophecy. We can cause our words to become reality. For example, let's assume that you and I know each other well. Suppose I decide one day that you don't like me. Maybe it was a look in your eye or something you said. I may even tell my wife my conclusions. She would most likely say that I was wrong, but I would undoubtedly remain convinced that I was right.

I would then begin to behave toward you as if you didn't

like me—perhaps ignore you, talk about you, or even ridicule you. At this point you would be alerted to my antisocial behavior and would conclude that I had some unfounded feelings toward you. In all likelihood, you would start to ignore me, talk about me, or even ridicule me. Then I would be absolutely certain you didn't like me, so I would return to my wife and say, "See, I told you so."

The mother of the clumsy boy guarantees his clumsiness by publicly announcing it and then expecting it. We all tend to act out the picture the Significant Other paints of us. Children tend to believe and act out what they are told.

During my live seminars on self-image, I ask the audience if someone has a spool of thread. And sure enough, someone always has one. I invite that person to join me on stage for a little experiment. I want to show everyone how strong I am to be able to break a strand of thread. That gets a laugh, since I stand 6'6" and weigh around 250 pounds.

I ask my helper to encircle me with one strand of thread and I break that easily. Then two and three and four. Somewhere around seven strands of thread, I become a prisoner, unable to break the chains that bind me. It was only a little strand of thread, yes, but one too many.

That shows why we have to be careful with our comments and be sensitive to others. We must show self-control even in the midst of personal pressure and tension. "So also the tongue is a small part of the body, and yet it boasts of great things. Behold, how great a forest is set aflame by such a small fire! But no one can tame the tongue; it is a restless evil and full of deadly poison" (James 3:5, 8).

Negative Conditioning

The second cause of a negative self-image is the fact that we are surrounded by people who think negatively. We have all been trained to think negatively. We are conditioned to see what is wrong with something rather than to see what is right. We are more likely to criticize people than to encourage them.

I have nothing against teaching children the need for self-discipline and self-control. But when this is exercised unreasonably and little people are unable to explore their world, their willingness to assert themselves will diminish. Parents should always seek to channel little children and young people into new situations and to encourage them in personal growth.

Just listen sometime to the vocabulary and language of our culture. It is predominately negative. Recently we were at a missions banquet which, unfortunately, was poorly attended. I heard one of the men in charge of the event say that the hall was half empty. I thought, "No it's not—it's half full." But our semantic emphasis is generally on the negative. Listen to the weather forecast and you will always hear that there is a 30 percent chance of rain, but you will never hear there is a 70 percent chance of sunshine. Then you have the teenager coming home from school, saying, "Boy, I'll never get my homework done." And guess what—he never gets it done. We are raised and socialized to think and emphasize the negative; and then we set out to fulfill our negative thinking.

That is one of the basic tensions in our culture today and it affects every fiber of our society. It brings tension to families as members try to prove others wrong and delight in exposing mistakes. It brings tension to churches as people compete for position. It brings tension to business life, where promotions are often based on the fewest failures rather than the most successes. Because we have things turned around, we spend most of our time looking for weaknesses rather than praising strengths.

Unfair Comparisons
The third major cause of a negative self-image is unfair comparison between ourselves and others.

There is perhaps no greater influence on our lives today than television. This medium has single-handedly been able to socialize us into gross feelings of inadequacy. Commercials are designed to portray the fantasy of perfection. When we watch them we are forced to agree that we are not at all like that which we see. We are then lured by the myth of what we can be, if we simply follow the directions. Unfortunately, once we purchase the fairy-tale product and follow the directions explicitly, we still don't turn into a gorgeous princess or a handsome prince, but remain tadpoles turning into bullfrogs.

Now that can be discouraging, as time after time, product after product, myth after myth, the search goes on. The Madison Avenue moguls make us feel terribly inferior by causing us to evaluate ourselves on a single dimension—that of appearance. Everything we are, they imply, is determined by our toothpaste, our hair spray, our soap, our automobile, our...and so it goes. How ridiculous!

From the cradle to the grave, we are bombarded with this superficial thinking. To counteract such stagnant reasoning, we need the balance which comes from accepting the values that God places on our appearance and on our abilities. We will always have feelings of inferiority if we use man's standard rather than God's. "Man looks at the outward appearance, but the Lord looks at the heart" (1 Samuel 16:7). The prophecy of Isaiah concerning the Messiah guarantees us that God is not at all concerned about physical beauty, but is measuring us by the character of Jesus Christ. "He hath no form nor comeliness; and when we shall see Him, there is no beauty that we should desire Him" (Isaiah 53:2, KJV).

Self-acceptance begins by recognizing that God prescribed the formula for us before we were born. "Thine eyes did see my substance, yet being unperfect; and in Thy book all my members were written, which in continuance were fashioned, when as yet there was none of them" (Psalm 139:16, KJV).

We can always correct those things which God leaves to us as choices. But about some things we have no choice; and we should make the best of them, especially physical characteristics we can do absolutely nothing about. In my seminars, I suggest that people memorize *The Serenity Prayer*:

God grant me the serenity
to accept the things I cannot change,
courage to change the things I can
and wisdom to know the difference.

Another unfair comparison we tend to make is based on life's experiences and opportunities. We look at others and ask, "Why can't I do that?" or "Why don't I have a college education?" Then we conclude that we are inferior to them. Each of us has drawn such conclusions from time to time, but they come from erroneous assumptions. The worst assumption we make is that we all have had the same opportunities. I have even heard motivational speakers tell audiences that this is true. It simply is not so. God created us to be unique. No two of us, not even brothers who grew up in the same home, are exactly alike; and therefore, they do not have the exact, same opportunities.

Life has been generous to me and I consider myself very fortunate to have been able to acquire the level of education I have. I never dreamed I would ever be a college professor. But a series of events and circumstances culminated in giving me the opportunity to attain four college degrees. I know that many people are impressed by education and consequently develop feelings of inferiority when in the presence of a Ph.D.

Right after my oral examinations, my thesis supervisor took me back to his office and put it all in perspective when he said, "Now, let's make a deal. I won't tell on you if you won't tell on me." In other words, there really is nothing to be in awe about. Some people just didn't have the opportunity to get a college education. But we all have the opportunity to do the very best we can with what we have.

The wisest man I ever knew was not a college professor nor was he a medical doctor, pastor, businessman, nor any other occupation generally associated with success. He was a farmer who never knew any other but to give his very best. He went to school only through grade five, and then lived at home longer than most boys in order to help his father out of a financial crisis. He left the farm in good hands, making sure his parents were well cared for, and then moved to the big city. He was full of honor and humility. He never thought too highly of himself, and lived by the simple formula, "It takes all your life to build your character and 30 seconds to lose it." He became a policeman and served with distinguished faithfulness for over 30 years. He never reached a high rank, but his name was known throughout the force for uncompromising integrity.

For the sake of his family, he emigrated to a foreign country. He was willing to leave behind his life and all that he knew for the benefit of his sons. He struggled and worked very hard the last years of his life as a prison guard and a janitor. His wife died only four months before their planned retirement. After he retired he became a visitation pastor in his home church and the people loved him. Why? He had seen life. He had lived through trials and tribulations. He was wise, not because of a formal education but because he knew God and walked with Him.

This wise man was my dad. The experiences of his life made it impossible for him to do certain things. Many times he felt inferior because of his limitations. But to his sons, Samuel S. Baird was a giant among men. The last time I heard him speak in church was in a prayer meeting the Wednesday before he died so suddenly. He simply stood and read his life's verse: "Stand fast therefore in the liberty wherewith Christ hath made us free, and be not entangled again with the yoke of bondage" (Galatians 5:1, KJV).

The following day he was going to visit my brother in Wheaton, Illinois. I drove him to the bus station, and as we chatted he reached over and grabbed my leg with the big hand I had grown so accustomed to and repeated a statement that I must have heard 100 times in my youth. "Son, always do what you know to be right and leave the consequences to God." His practice in all things was cooperation without compromise.

It is unfair to compare ourselves to others without remembering that the experiences we face make us each uniquely different. A couple of years ago, Donna and I visited several tribal mission stations in South America, observing the work projects in which our summer missionaries were involved. We were exposed to some fascinating cultures and spent a lot of time with primitive peoples. One of the highlights was a hunting trip in the jungles of Bolivia, with a group of Ayore Indians. The Indians took our team, a few members at a time, into the jungle to track wild boar, armadillo, turtle, and anything else that happened along the way, including a jaguar. Needless to say, we were exhausted at the end of the day. We were also mesmerized by these Indians who seemed to float effortlessly between the vines and thorns and with instant decision strike the one machete blow necessary to clear the path. We were torn by the thorns and never did figure out how to clear the path, no matter how many swings of the machete we took.

When evening came and the jungle sounds began to fill the night like an orchestra preparing for a performance, it all seemed so eerie. During the night, sleep seemed to escape me. I remember looking out from under my mosquito net at the stars in the southern sky and thinking, "Isn't it hard to believe that I could be in this hostile place, with my three oldest children and other summer missionaries, lying beside these primitive tribesmen? Wouldn't it be incredible if these Indians left us here in the middle of the jungle? We would be lost." Not only could we not have found our way out, but we wouldn't have been able to survive in an environment that seemed so hostile. When our matches ran out, we would not have had fires. When the small food supply was gone, we would have had real difficulty in tracking jungle prey. It would likely have ended in tragedy.

Now, should we conclude that the Ayore Indians are smarter than we are? Would we be correct in thinking we are stupid? No, certainly not. Nor would we be able to claim that the Ayore tribesmen were dumb, if we were to parachute them into the downtown area of a major city. They would be out of their environment, as we were. We would both be confused because our experiences in life had not prepared us for the situation.

The one rule we should remember is this: whatever we are able to accomplish, we should strive for with every ounce of courage and energy. We should always do the best we can.

Another unfortunate tendency that comes from comparison is to conclude that if we fail in one situation or event, we are failures! Our society has made much out of winning and losing at sports, and always defines these in black and white terms. From that background, we apply the same reasoning to other situations. If we are not selected for the high school basketball team, the cheerleading squad, or the band, we do not view the refusal in terms of the "selection process" but more as a "rejection process." In our feelings of being forsaken or rejected, we magnify our woes and slip into depression and discouragement.

It is during these times that we are most vulnerable to seeing ourselves as failures. On these occasions we need to remind ourselves of history's entourage of successful failures. All progress in the world has been made by men and women who were willing to march across the battleground of dismal failure, facing every trial known to man, to arrive on the other side with the glint of victory in their eyes. The only thing which kept most of them going was vision and hope. "Where there is no vision, the people perish" (Proverbs 29:18, KJV).

Not long ago I was flying from Orlando to a large northern city. I had tried everything I could to get a seat in the bulkhead but that didn't work. The stewardess at the gate recommended a seat in the exit row. It was a center seat and I must confess I was not looking forward to the flight.

Early in the trip I got my briefcase out and began to work on this book. Seated by the window was a young lady who asked what I was writing. I told her my book was about self-image. As we talked, it became clear why I was in that seat—she was hurting from her past. Now 20 years old, she had been on her own since she was 17. She was from a Christian home, or at least one where they attended church on Sunday. She began to share with me the pressures of her adolescence and the peculiar demands her father placed on the children regarding their ability in mathematics. His work demanded a very sophisticated use of math, and he measured the scholastic ability of his children in terms of their math profile. He was using himself as the standard of excellence and expecting nothing less from his children. One evening, when this girl was 15, her father tyrannically demanded that she be able to do a certain section of homework. After she tried for a while, she realized she was unable to do it. Anticipating the fury of her father, she panicked and thought, "I'm a failure." Because she concluded life was not worth living, she took every pill she could find in the house. She survived, but was deeply scarred emotionally. Since that time, she has wandered to and fro looking for love, security, and understanding.

Many people label themselves as failures because they are unsuccessful in one area of life.

What a joy and comfort it is to know our Creator in an intimate way, and to be sure He is not done molding us, and that He knows how to finish the job right. "We are His workmanship" (Ephesians 2:10).

"O Lord...forsake not the works of Thine own hands" (Psalm 138:8, KJV).

A Poor Memory

The fourth major cause of a negative self-image is a poor memory. Students from grade school to graduate school face one common denominator—exams. The emphasis of examinations seems to remain constant, even though the educational philosophy changes. Examinations generally test us not on what we know but rather on what we can remember about what we know.

If you know anything about poultry, and chickens in particular, you know there is a pecking order in the coop. Without going into details as to how that hierarchy is established, let me say that every chicken knows who he can peck and likewise who can peck him. When a new bird is added, it doesn't take long till he is placed in the order of things. On very cold nights you will notice that those of the lowest order are on the outer layers making sure those of higher rank are kept warm.

In like manner, but with more complexity, school classrooms have a pecking order. The hierarchy is established on such variables as grades, sports, looks, and personality. Athletic ability and an outgoing personality are the result of one's self-confidence. One early cause of self-confidence in school appears to be scholastic ability. Grades have always been a separator in school, and therefore we need to find ways to improve the grades of young people.

All too vividly I recall horrifying moments in a classroom when a teacher handed back exams, not alphabetically (which I enjoyed), but by grade. The worst kind of teacher would also announce the grade each received. In such a setting, it isn't long before the group resembles a coop. The intellectuals become an elite corps who parade all the way through school on their performance history.

In case it may sound like an overstatement, let me make a confession as a former professor. Not only does the class resemble a coop, but teachers use pigeon holes to categorize students. After giving my first midterm exams, I carefully graded the students. But after a while, I began to think of them according to their grades. I feel I actually limited them on all future exams to a very narrow range around their first grades. Why? Because that is what I expected from them and we want to see our expectations fulfilled.

Doing well on examinations requires a good memory. To acquire a good to excellent memory does not require practice or even much discipline. It is available to everyone.

I have a good time with large audiences when I tell them that I can teach them in only ten minutes how to have a phenomenal memory. There are always those who don't believe they can do it. After having some fun by overimpressing them with my fantastic ability to memorize, I set about to show them how. In ten minutes the audience has discovered the secret to a good memory. To remember facts, all you need is something to trigger your memory and to release back to you the thoughts you placed in your memory bank. But it requires the use of a system. Once you learn the system you can confidently tackle exams and other memory feats with ease.

There are a number of systems available and they all are based on association. An orderly progression of items is associated with a number which becomes the trigger mechanism to unlock the material associated with the item. I encourage you to use a memory system. Some are better than others, but they all will work.

Let me close with this thought. As wonderful as it is to have a good memory, it is a blessing to know there are those who are willing to forget.

When you take a look at these causes of a negative self-image, you can understand why so many people with ability, skill, and great potential flounder through life. As we outline the cure for a negative self-image in the next chapter, we will identify ways for you to help yourself and others develop a positive self-image.

"In all these things we overwhelmingly conquer through Him who loved us" (Romans 8:37). Absolutely nothing can separate us from the love of God, which is in Christ Jesus our Lord. Go on, I dare you. Be a conqueror!

4

Cure for a Negative Self-Image

"I will lift up mine eyes unto the hills, from whence cometh my help" (Psalm 121:1, KJV).

I don't have many talents and skills in the area of construction and carpentry and this bothers me at times. However, I am always impressed with others who are skilled carpenters. I am writing this book on a magnificent credenza with cupboards and built-in bookshelves. I use it as my desk and work center and never cease to be amazed at the simple yet intricate design. It was built by my good friend, Matt Castagna. Matt and his wife, Leslie, are presently living in our missionary apartment on the church property waiting to open up a new mission field for World Outreach Fellowship in South America.

It is hard to believe the transformation their apartment underwent, after construction of new kitchen cupboards and a built-in table. Everything seems to fit perfectly. I am especially impressed with doors that have perfect corners and swing easily on their hinges. Certainly, if I had been the carpenter, this would not be the case.

A group of our summer missionaries went to the country of Belize to survey the needs of tribal people. During their exploits into the jungles, they would often come across a Mayan ruin. Just as the pyramids of Egypt, the Mayan construction is a truly amazing phenomenon. Every rock fits perfectly into place—each one individually hewn to do a very special job. No rock, once chiseled and sculptured, could fit in any other location.

That is exactly what God wants for His children. God is anxious to fit us into His church as living stones:

> So then you are no longer strangers and aliens, but you are fellow-citizens with the saints, and are of God's household, having been built upon the foundation of the apostles and prophets, Christ Jesus Himself being the cornerstone, in whom the whole building, being fitted together is growing into a holy temple in the Lord; in whom you also are being built together into a dwelling of God in the Spirit   (Ephesians 2:19-22).

Notice verse 21: "In whom the whole building, being fitted together is growing into a holy temple in the Lord." What kinds of stones are used to build a temple or a huge pyramid? Big stones, little stones, and even odd-shaped stones are essential, if they all fit together. Can you see the picture? Our Lord is the Master Builder who orders the stone masons to chip away at each rock until He makes it a perfect fit.

Little stones will have to be satisfied filling in the gaps. Big stones will have to be willing to endure the stress and be responsible for the support of others. Odd-shaped stones will need to be patient, waiting for the right spot for service.

The Lord has a chosen spot and is anxious that we be willing to fit in. Some of us may be placed underground never to be seen, in order that the foundation will be secure. But we must never crave to be the cornerstone. Without the proper cornerstone the building would fall, and this spot is reserved for the Lord Jesus Christ.

For the many years I worked as an industrial psychologist I was aware that one of the continuing plagues for management in many industries is the high turnover ratio. Recent research statistics show that over 80 percent of the people working full time are dissatisfied with their employment. The specific reasons for this problem are too complex for discussion here. But in general terms, we can say that most people are unhappy with life. Some people are unhappy because they want to do more; some want to do less; still others are constantly searching for new opportunities and careers—wanting to do something else.

Let me hasten to add that dissatisfaction is not the private province of the non-Christian world. Many Christians never see a clear picture of what their purpose really is and therefore get as frustrated as everyone else. We are all looking for the perfect fit. We are all searching for our special niche. But we will not find that spot until we recognize what our primary purpose is. We were created to glorify God. In speaking to His Father the Lord Jesus prayed, "I glorifed Thee on the earth, having accomplished the work which Thou hast given Me to do" (John 17:4).

The basic cure for a negative self-image is to come to grips with the need to know God's will for your life. For the Christian, success is not only knowing God's will but also walking in it. It doesn't matter whether God has called us to be big stones, little stones, or odd-shaped stones. What He desires from us is that we glorify Him.

When the Apostle Paul wrote his letter to the church at Colosse, he was writing to his spiritual grandchildren. Paul had never been to Colosse, but he was intensely interested in their spiritual development. So much so that he gives us a formula of how to pray for the spiritual maturity of our children or other loved ones. The only long-lasting cure for a negative self-image is spiritual growth:

You learned it from Epaphras, our beloved fellow bond-servant, who is a faithful servant of Christ on our behalf, and he also informed us of your love in the Spirit. For this reason also, since the day we heard of it, we have not ceased to pray for you and to ask that you may be filled with the knowledge of His will in all spiritual wisdom and understanding, so that you may walk in a manner worthy of the Lord, to please Him in all respects, bearing fruit in every good work and increasing in the knowledge of God; strengthened with all power, according to His glorious might, for the attaining of all steadfastness and patience; joyously giving thanks to the Father, who has qualified us to share in the inheritance of the saints in light (Colossians 1:7-12).

In verse 9 Paul says that he wants them to "be filled with the knowledge of His will in all spiritual wisdom and understanding." Paul is emphasizing the critical need to truly understand God's will, so that we may walk worthy, be faithful, increase in the knowledge of God, be strong, be steadfast and patient, and be thankful.

Knowing God's Will

To know God's Will = Good Testimony + Soul Winner + Daily Bible Study + Inner Strength + Stability + Patience + Thankfulness.

How did Jesus glorify the Father? Let us look at John 17:4 again: "I glorified Thee on earth, having accomplished the work which Thou hast given Me to do." Jesus glorified the Father by completing the task which He was given—of being the chief cornerstone. The path which this demanded took Him from the cradle to the cross. Likewise, we glorify the Father, or do His will for our lives, if we accomplish the work He has given to us.

What is the work He has assigned to us? If the Lord Jesus is both the cornerstone and the essential sacrifice for God's redemptive plan for humanity, what is left for us to do? What is our work?

The Lord Jesus has assigned us the task of sharing God's redemptive plan with the whole world. The very last words our Lord said on earth were, "But you shall receive power when the Holy Spirit has come upon you; and you shall be

My witnesses both in Jerusalem, and in all Judea and Samaria, and even to the remotest part of the earth" (Acts 1:8). Therefore, our work is to take the Gospel of Jesus Christ to the ends of the earth.

We cannot be aware of God's will, however, until we are aware of who God is. Hudson Taylor, the great missionary to China, had this plaque hanging on the wall of his home in West China, "The Sun stood still, The Iron did float, this God is our God." God answered the prayer of an ordinary man and stayed the sun. God suspended the law of gravity and made an iron axe float (Joshua 10:13; 2 Kings 6:6). This is the God to whom we come. This is the God whose promises we count on. He is the *El Shaddai,* the One who is enough.

To better understand who God is, it is helpful to consider some of the names of God.

● JEHOVAH-NISSI—I am thy banner. "He brought me into the banqueting house, and His banner over me was love" (Song of Solomon 2:4, KJV).

● JEHOVAH-SHALOM—I am thy peace. "And the peace of God, which passeth all understanding, shall keep your hearts and minds through Christ Jesus" (Philippians 4:7, KJV).

● JEHOVAH-TSIDKENDU—I am thy righteousness. "If you know that He is righteous, you know that everyone also who practices righteousness is born of Him" (1 John 2:29).

● JEHOVAH-JIREH—I am the One who provides. "The Lord is my shepherd, I shall not want" (Psalm 23:1).

● JEHOVAH-RAPHA—I am the One who heals. "Weeping may last for the night, but a shout of joy comes in the morning" (Psalm 30:5).

● JEHOVAH-RA-AH—I am thy Shepherd. "The good Shepherd lays down His life for the sheep" (John 10:11).

● JEHOVAH-SHAMMAH—I am the One who is there. "When thou passest through the waters, I will be with thee; and through the rivers, they shall not overflow thee; when thou walkest through the fire, thou shall not be burned; neither shall the flame kindle upon thee" (Isaiah 43:2, KJV).

There is an expression in industrial psychology which refers to principles of employee selection—The Past is Prologue. The past is the best indication of how anyone will perform in the future. So it is with our unchanging God. His truth makes it impossible for Him to lie. His omniscience makes it impossible for Him to be deceived. His omnipotence means He has power to do whatever is within His purposes.

Doing God's Will

The ultimate cure for a negative self-image is to know God's will and to realize that you are a special person to Him. You are uniquely fitted to the job He has given you. What are the results when you know God's will and desire to follow it?

● A worthy walk. Did you ever notice that basketball players, especially the stars, have a special walk? They seem to bounce along. Football players, on the other hand, seem to devour the sidewalk. There are mannerisms attached to certain groups of people. Athletes walk one way, policemen walk another, postmen walk yet another. They are revealing their vocations whether they want to or not, because they simply can't help it.

We have a family dog named Muffin who is a purebred Lhasa apso. He's a cute little fellow with shaggy long hair. When Muffin walks he seems to strut with arrogance. But he can't do anything about this—it is part of his pedigree, his heritage.

Likewise it is our heritage as the family of God to carry distinguishing signs with us. We will walk worthy of the high calling and bear a good testimony for our Lord.

● Fruitful living. It is a fact that apple trees produce apples and orange trees produce oranges, and that's the way it will always be. Scripture says, "The tree is known by its fruit" (Matthew 12:33). Once you have really caught the passion for the job you have been called to, you will seize every opportunity to glorify God by presenting His great redemption plan.

We are to bloom where we are planted. The Lord's plan is for each of us to look after the home front first.

What are you doing for the Lord today? Are you involved in the work He called you to do? If you will perform the unique role He has assigned to you, never again will you question your ability or your self-image.

• Increased knowledge of God. I must admit that the greatest battle I fight in my life is consistency in my fellowship time with the Lord. But I learned a long time ago that it is easy to blame the devil for this battle when it is really my flesh and my will that keep me from meditating on God's Word. How amazing it is that we find time for everything else but our quiet time alone with Him.

Our lack of time with the Lord each day is both a bad habit and an act of the will. Habits are the result of practice, drill, and rehearsal. If you want to be good at anything, you must be willing to practice, drill, and rehearse. It will not happen overnight, but it will happen if you are consistent. Many people want to have a greater knowledge of the Word. Still others want to be men and women of great faith. But they are not willing to pay the price. Some say, "I'd do anything to be like that,"—anything but what it takes. For what it takes is the discipline of follow-through.

If more people spent time with God in prayer and in the study of His Word, there would be less struggle with negative self-image. If God is for us, who then can be against us? Of whom shall we be afraid?

• Strength and power. It is comforting to know that I don't have to depend solely on myself for my sustenance and strength. Many people who suffer from a negative self-image are afraid of responsibility. It is as though they feel totally alone and without help. As believers, we are not alone, even though the enemy is anxious to stir our emotions with such a thought. God's Word is filled with promises to His children. Each one of us is a unique "living stone."

The strength of the Lord truly gives us the strength to attempt new things, to initiate programs, to face embarrassment, to be willing to fail, to face new situations, and to realize that we are not odd because we feel inadequate. Remember Paul's declaration to the world, "I can do all things through Him who strengthens me" (Philippians 4:13).

• Steadfastness and patience. One of the greatest stories in the Bible is about Joseph. Even after the cruel manner in which his brothers sold him as a slave, he waited patiently in Egypt praying for his family. He was steadfast in his loyalty to God and he protected his testimony. Because he did not harbor hatred in his heart, God honored him so that he became prime minister of Egypt.

Joseph never forgot who he was. Being forsaken by his brothers did not mean he had been forsaken by God. Joseph remained faithful, not because of his position in Egypt, but because of his position as a child of the King of glory. His self-image was never in doubt; he knew who he was. He knew that although men would do evil against him, God would use everything for good. Joseph patiently waited because he trusted God to fulfill His plan.

God desires for you to be willing to be fitted perfectly into place. Are you ready for service?

• Thankfulness. In the fall of 1981, three other men and I founded a new mission society, World Outreach Fellowship (WOF), Longwood, Florida. Paul Johnson and his wife, Robin, had been missionaries in Bolivia contacting primitive, nomadic tribes. Matt Castagna had also been involved in a similar ministry for several years and David Sanford had grown up as a PK turned MK.

The early thrust of WOF is in SPRINT (Summer Projects in the Tribes). This summer mission program challenges young people to travel overseas with a team to help tribal missionaries build airstrips in the jungle, clinics, homes, and whatever else is required to assist them reach hidden peoples for Christ.

You can be certain that our team members return with a greater vision. One word that comes from them time and time again is thankfulness: "We have so much to be thankful for," "We can be thankful that in God's providence we were born here," and so forth. It is interesting to note that many tribal languages do not have a word for thankfulness. Why? Thankfulness is a spiritual principle.

I have noticed an increasing tendency today away from saying "Thank you." Adults mutter "Uh-huh" under their breath and children don't say anything. Paul warned Timothy that in the last days, "Men will be lovers of self, lovers of money, boastful, arrogant, revilers, disobedient to parents, ungrateful, unholy" (2 Timothy 3:2). Yet as we mature in the Lord, we become more grateful for everything we have and also for not having many things.

A worthy walk, fruitful living, an increased knowledge of God, strength and power, steadfastness and patience, and thankfulness will result in your life once you recognize that you are to glorify the Father by completing the task to which you were assigned. We were each given the job of fitting in perfectly to share God's redemptive plan with a lost world.

Hasten the Cure

What has all this got to do with negative self-image? Individuals are imprisoned in a negative self-image because they do not have a purpose and because they do not feel needed or essential. The most important calling in all the world is to the vocation of "making disciples." And this gives both purpose and a sureness of being needed.

Here are some practical suggestions to hasten the cure of a negative self-image.

● Help other people. Keep your eyes and ears open for people in need. Kids, help your parents. Men, don't be embarrassed to give a lady your chair. Husbands, don't forget to seat your wives at the dinner table. Oh, these are such little things, but life is full of little things and they count.

You will be amazed what will happen to your attitude, and you will notice a positive impact on others too. If you genuinely become more helpful, you will be a success by any standard.

• GIGO. This is a buzz word from computer technology which means Garbage In—Garbage Out (GIGO). Because a computer is limited to what is put in, it can only give what it has already received. In a parallel way, we must protect our minds to the degree that it is possible. This means controlling our reading and our viewing. The eyes are the "windows of the soul."

Some time ago I was conducting a seminar in Buffalo, New York. For a break at the noon hour, I went back to my room and decided to watch television for a little while. The soaps were on—something I hadn't seen in over 20 years. What a change! Such depravity and flagrant abuses to the mind. The subtle thing about these programs is that they creep up on you until you begin to believe that this is what life is like.

• Act as if you can. William James, the father of modern psychology, suggests this principle as a means of personal growth. The concept encourages us to visualize ourselves doing what we want to do and then to mimic those who are already doing it.

Part of the "Act as if" principle demands a careful study of what is happening. You must examine what is being said, and how, and what the individual speaking or acting looks like. You would not expect a cowboy to ride broncos wearing a pinstripe suit. Nor would you expect a stockbroker to sound like a TV wrestler. We all have certain role expectations. Dress for the role and the occasion. Act appropriately. You never get a second chance to make a first impression.

• Work hard. There is integrity in hard work, and people respect those who give 110 percent. However, many people are trying to fight World War III with Civil War weapons. Be sure you are equipped for what you want to do. There is no sense feeling frustrated when you have not done what needs to be done. If you want to be a doctor, you must pay the price of training. If you want to be a contractor, you must pay the price of experience. Whatever you do, work hard and give it your best.

Insure the Cure

Just because you win one battle does not mean the war is over. Simply because you defeat a negative self-image today does not guarantee it won't raise its ugly head tomorrow. It most assuredly will. Satan will not give up easily because he knows that we are essential in God's plan to redeem the world. How then can we ward off the assaults? There is only one way—through prayer. "The effectual, fervent prayer of a righteous man availeth much" (James 5:16, KJV). The condition to the fulfillment of this prayer is righteousness. This demands holy living. The Lord gave two principles of prayer.

● God's patience. Even though God desires to do a certain thing, He often waits until men pray. The greatest example of God not exercising His will or desire is salvation itself. God loves everyone and desires that no one should perish. Yet He waits for men to pray.

● Our persistence. God is asking us, "Do you really mean it? Are you committed to this? Are you in earnest? Can you do without this request being answered? Or is it something you must have at all costs?" John Knox, the great Scottish reformer, prayed, "Give me Scotland or I die." Moses prayed that if God would not blot out the sin of Israel, He would blot out Moses' name (Exodus 32:32).

There are many biblical examples of persistence. Naaman had to dip seven times in the Jordan. Why not only once? The Children of Israel had to walk around Jericho 13 times, and as if that weren't enough, they had to blow trumpets. Before the promised Holy Spirit came to the church, 120 people prayed for 10 days. Persistence is essential for answered prayer.

The cure for a negative self-image lies in understanding God's will for your life. God expects you to employ those skills and talents He has given you. Do not neglect God's Word or faithfulness in prayer. There are many imitation cures available today, but they will not last. A negative self-image will be cured permanently only through spiritual growth.

5

Characteristics
of a Healthy
Self-Image—I

The little black boy became more and more excited as he waited outside the locker room door of the Los Angeles Coliseum. He was waiting for the Cleveland Browns to finish their game against the Los Angeles Rams. Like many boys his age, he idolized Jimmy Brown, the great running back of Cleveland.

Suddenly he appeared, larger than life, and the little boy nervously blurted out, "Hey, Mr. Brown, you're my hero."

Brown, engrossed in thought, merely discarded the comment he had heard so often with, "Yeah, kid."

But the little guy persisted, craving some recognition as he jogged alongside of him. "Mr. Brown, I have all your records and pictures pinned up in my room."

And, Brown, still hardly noticing the boy, grunted out another, "Yeah, kid."

With a growing tenacity the boy finally got Jimmy Brown's attention when he said, "Yeah, Mr. Brown, I know all your records by heart. And, Mr. Brown, I'm going to beat every one of them."

Jimmy Brown stopped, fixed his eyes on the boy and asked, "Hey, kid, what's your name?"

The little boy smiled and replied, "Simpson, sir. My friends call me O.J." And the rest, of course, is history.

The average age for being named to *Who's Who in America* is 27. It's a fact that early in life we form patterns of success or failure. These patterns do not simply become evident when we get our first job but are a part of our environmental heritage.

David, the shepherd boy, just didn't know any better than to trust the Lord to see the great giant Goliath defeated. David appeared indignant and even confused at the attitudes of the soldiers of Israel, when he asked, "Who is this guy, who is this heathen, that he should even think about defying the armies of the living God?" (See 1 Samuel 17:26.) David argued with his brothers, pleaded with the king, and turned the job over to the Lord. David had already field-tested his faith with the lion and the bear, and he knew that old Goliath didn't stand a chance against the Lord of hosts.

David's heritage included many spiritual lessons. He knew beyond a shadow of a doubt that the battle was the Lord's. He placed his confidence in God's hands when he said, "This day will the Lord deliver you up into my hands ... that all the earth may know that there is a God in Israel" (17:46).

As we discuss the 12 characteristics of a strong and healthy self-image, a parallel could be drawn on each of them to the life of David. Each characteristic was demonstrated during the confrontation with Goliath.

Discipline

"I don't mean to say I am perfect. I haven't learned all I should even yet, but I keep working toward that day when I will finally be all that Christ saved me for and wants me to be.

"No, dear brothers, I am still not all I should be but I am bringing all my energies to bear on this one thing: Forgetting the past and looking forward to what lies ahead, I strain to reach the end of the race and receive the prize for which God is calling us up to heaven because of what Christ Jesus did for us " (Philippians 3:12-14, TLB).

In these few verses the Apostle Paul shares with us four actions which demand rugged discipline:

• Bringing all my energies to bear on one thing. Here Paul is declaring the need to focus on one thing. So many times we are distracted by other potential opportunities that we never get the original job done.

Henry Ford, the great inventor, was often asked, "How can I make my life a success?" He would always reply, "If you start something, finish it!"

Have you ever noticed how many good reasons there seem to be for quitting a job or a project? Or have you noticed how many times you have to fight the desire to procrastinate. Tomorrow—oh, there is always tomorrow.

Mr. Ford liked to tell the story of the time he was feverishly building his first car. He was working long hours in a little brick building behind his home, and his level of enthusiasm always seemed to run at the maximum. Then the thrill of it disappeared. Why? He had gone far enough on the first car to see how he could build the second one even better. So why spend all that time finishing a car that he already knew was inferior?

But something inside him pressed him on, as if realizing that he must totally focus on one thing—finishing what he started. In addition to discovering this fantastic principle, he learned more and more about the second car by finishing every detail of his original dream. If he had succumbed to the temptation of quitting on the first one, he might never have made a car at all. It requires discipline to keep our attention on one thing at a time.

• Forgetting the past. It is natural for us to look back and remember problems, thus inhibiting our willingness to go forward. We must discipline ourselves away from this basic inclination. Paul urges us to stop conjuring up past failures and using them as reasons for not attempting new opportunities.

• Looking forward. The writer to the Hebrews captures the thought this way: "Let us also lay aside every encumbrance, and the sin which so easily entangles us, and let us run with endurance the race that is set before us, fixing our eyes on Jesus, the author and perfector of faith" (Hebrews 12:1-2).

Discipline is required if we are to keep our eyes on the goal. It takes a steady gaze to keep focused on a vision. No matter what else happens, keep your eyes on the Lord.

Just before we left Northern Ireland for Canada, my dad took me one last time to visit the little farm where he was born. As we walked along the country road in County Down, he told me stories about his childhood. In his latter years, he often returned, in his daydreams, to this small but significant piece of real estate.

That same day he took me out to what remained of his boyhood home. What had once been a cozy, thatched cottage, complete with a bellows, fireplace, and hearth, was now overgrown with weeds. The mud walls still stood a couple of feet high, but most everything else was gone.

As we walked out in the field behind the home, he told me how he used to enjoy plowing. He taught me many lessons that day, most of which I came to understand years later. For example, he told of the extreme importance of the first furrow plowed in the field. He explained that every other furrow would be straight only if the first one was, since it was used as the standard, to give alignment and direction to the rest. That truth can certainly be applied to many areas of living, such as raising children. How important it is to set the pattern of love and discipline with the first child. Or perhaps we should all see ourselves as the first furrow in every field and desire that our lives set an example for others.

In order to get the furrow straight, Dad would have to keep the head of the horse in direct line with the big oak tree at the end of the field. Then he asked me, "Clifford, what do you think would have happened to the furrow if I had looked to the left or to the right or looked behind me?"

I really didn't know then, but I do now—the furrow would have been something other than a straight line. And that's the principle Paul was talking about in "Looking forward" or the writer of Hebrews when he said, "Looking unto Jesus." We must keep our eyes fixed on our goal. If we don't, we will wander aimlessly in life searching for direction. But fixing on the goal requires real discipline. Just as David the shepherd boy kept his faith and trust firmly rooted in the Lord of hosts, so he disciplined himself to keep his eyes on the forehead of the giant Goliath. His brothers and the other soldiers of Israel said, "Goliath's too big to fight." But David, who didn't know any better, said, "He's too big to miss."

● Straining to reach the end. The words *strain* and *press* carry with them the indication of hard work demanding strenuous effort. Anything that has worth always costs you something. It is true that there is no gain without pain.

Today people seem to have a craze for clubhouse exercising. We have seen the rise of health spas in big cities and small towns. Whether it is housewives rolling on their living room floors or professional athletes doing calisthenics, all exercise programs have one thing in common—there is no gain without pain. Regardless how many or how few sit-ups you do, there will be no benefit to your body until you reach the one that makes you groan.

It is only natural to resist pain. It is only natural to desire things which do not require discipline. Yet how vital it is for us to reach beyond our grasp, to dream dreams that refuse to be accomplished by idle hands. Have you ever noticed how some people are always behind until it's time to quit? What a man is depends largely on what he does when he has nothing to do.

Vision
"Where there is no vision the people run wild" (Proverbs 29:18, BERK).

Vision, in the context of this verse, means insight into spiritual things. I once saw this sign on a professor's wall: "Eyes that look are common, but eyes that see are rare." I have often thought how that describes most of us.

Donna and I assign specific household duties and responsibilities to each of our children. We make sure to vary the chores on a rotating basis, just to be certain they are handled equitably. When our youngest son, Bradley, is assigned to garbage detail, it never ceases to amaze me how often he fails to see a bulging green garbage bag in the middle of the kitchen floor. It is as though the sound of my voice is essential to activate his eyes.

Most of us face this malady in a variety of ways. The vision of many people is hampered by the debris left behind from past experiences. Some people are totally unwilling to think beyond the present, as though some dark foreboding cloud loomed on the horizon. God holds us responsible, not for what we have, but for what we could have; not for what we are, but for what we might be.

There is a wonderful story told of a young boy who was sitting on a wharf. He was fascinated by watching an old man fishing off the end of the pier. He began to notice that the old man was throwing away the larger fish and keeping the smaller ones. The little boy couldn't understand that, since he thought the whole object was to catch fish as big as possible. When he could stand it no more, he asked the old man why he was throwing away the big fish and keeping the small ones. The old man looked at him and said, "Son, my frying pan is only seven inches wide."

We are sometimes unable to look beyond our seven-inch circumstances to seize the opportunities which could be ours. David saw the awesome size of Goliath, but he also saw the Lord.

Satan's goal is to deceive every Christian into believing that with God all things are *not* possible. Satan wants us to focus on present trials and thus to diffuse the energy that we should be putting into our ministry.

Wisdom
"The fear of the Lord is the beginning of knowledge; fools despise wisdom and instruction" (Proverbs 1:7).

Shortly after my 16th birthday, my father taught me how to drive an automobile. He was very particular about all the details of when and how to accelerate, how to parallel park, maintaining the speed limit, and so forth. One day as we were going down to the bottom of our hill, a young girl drove through a stop sign right in front of us. I really got upset. I laid on the horn and chewed her out but good. There was just one problem—she didn't hear any of it. My father did though, and after I had carried on long enough, Dad said, "Clifford, do you realize that girl has had total control over you for the last five minutes?" What a picture of life—spending time and emotional energy over circumstances about which we have no control. Even when we have learned the lesson many times, we keep on repeating the error.

Wisdom is defined as the best use of knowledge. Knowledge by itself does not produce wisdom; but if we apply knowledge effectively, we are wise. Here is a psychological principle which most people don't realize. *We do not do the things we know. We only do the things we believe.* There are many folks who have plenty of head knowledge but are not willing or motivated to apply it. We believe the things we have experienced. We can hear dozens of people share their experiences, but it is not until we are willing to take the step of faith and apply what we know to our own lives that we really believe.

As I travel the country, putting on sales and management seminars, I have met thousands of well-meaning people who have attended every seminar that's ever come to town, but who have never really changed. What are they looking for? What magic formula are they expecting? They are not wise for they are not willing to apply the knowledge they already have. We see the same problem acted out Sunday after Sunday in church. There are those who refuse to apply spiritual principles to their lives. They are not void of knowledge but of diligence. From message after message, class after class, their knowledge grows and their lives become hardened. It is a terrifying thought that one day God will look out over the portals of heaven and decide that enough is enough. The psalmist records the terror of that moment this way, "And He gave them their request; but sent leanness into their soul" (Psalm 106:15, KJV).

If we are to live in the "fear of the Lord," we must actively participate in and follow those things we know to be true. Those principles which are taught clearly in the Word of God demand an obedience which comes from a servant's heart. The very same consideration must be applied to every area of life—business, family, social, and church life. Proven principles for success demand active obedience. If we merely "know" them but do not apply them, we are worse than fools.

Decision
"Commit your works to the Lord, and your plans will be established" (Proverbs 16:3).

One of Walt Disney's favorite stories was about the young boy who tried to get into the circus parade. From the time he heard that the circus was coming to town, he determined to be a part of the parade. But he was unsuccessful in his attempts until he read a sign in a store window: "Trombone player needed for the circus band—see the bandmaster." He got the job.

On the day of the parade the streets were crowded, balloons and streamers were in the air and excitement was high. Just as the band was making the turn to head up through the town square, the bandmaster heard an awful sound. He raced back and discovered the noise was coming from the trombone. In a fit of embarrassment and anger he shouted at the boy, "I thought you could play the trombone!" To which the startled little guy replied, "How did I know I couldn't? I never tried it before!"

One quality that separates successful people from unsuccessful is a willingness to make decisions. Decision-making is not dependent on having all the facts. The ability to make decisions is dependent on how much we want to move. It is rather like the turtle. Regardless of how slowly the turtle moves, if he wants to go anywhere, he has to stick his neck out. Making decisions always leaves you vulnerable since there is risk involved. Obviously some decisions have greater consequences than others, but they all require an inner strength and willingness to be responsible for your actions.

Most people resist making decisions because of one or more of the following fears:

• Fear of Rejection: Because of a basic need to be loved and accepted, we are very susceptible to peer pressure. This phenomenon is not the exclusive preserve of teenagers, for every one of us is greatly influenced by friends. Peer pressure is not always negative. There can be positive effects so long as we are being influenced by the right kind of people.

One evening as I left Chicago on the last flight back to Orlando, I found myself getting really annoyed at four young men who were already well tanked up for their week in the sun. They were noisy and they were rude. They were boisterous and made inappropriate comments. And frankly, I was tired and longing for some peace and quiet and some shuteye on the way home. Such was not to be the case.

I was sitting in the bulkhead aisle and they were about four rows behind me, singing, shouting, and whistling at the stewardesses. Then one of the guys spotted a girl who was sitting by herself right behind me. He sat down beside her and began to ask her questions. At first she ignored him until he turned very charming. Before long they were making plans to see each other during the week, at parties and other activities. The two of them were soon joined by the other guys, and plans were wrapped up for a really wild week.

I was fascinated at this study of human behavior. While we waited for our luggage, I couldn't resist an opportunity to talk to the girl, who was an RN. I told her who I was and then asked what it was that allowed her to make herself immediately vulnerable to people she had never met. Her answer didn't surprise me. She admitted to having difficulty ignoring people and was afraid of "offending" them. She said she thought it would be a relief from boredom to see them during the week. She was fully aware of the demands she would face but didn't want to hurt their feelings. Now that is peer pressure in the raw!

• Fear of Failure. People who suffer from this fear are lacking clear objectives in life. The individual who fears failure learns that if he never sets a goal or makes a commitment to excel, he cannot fail. This is carried into every facet of his life.

People who suffer from this fear do not know from one day to the next what they are going to do. They don't plan, they don't organize, they don't commit, they don't seek new opportunities. They generally pursue routine idleness.

Decision-makers have already faced the reality that they will make mistakes. All of their decisions do not turn out as planned, but this does not deter them from pressing on and on. Failures are merely new opportunities to apply knowledge.

We should not allow failure in one situation to rob us of success in another. There is a great illustration of this in Acts 8. Philip was enjoying a fruitful ministry in the city of Samaria. Simon the sorcerer was one of his followers and Philip did not discern that Simon's motives were less than spiritual. Peter, however, recognized that he was a phony.

A little while later an angel of the Lord spoke to Philip and told him to go into the burning desert, on the road to Gaza. We read that he arose and went. He did not say, "Lord, I don't think I can do the job anymore. I should have discerned Simon's problem. I don't think You should trust me anymore. I just don't feel adequate." Philip did not allow Satan to crush him with his failure, but rather put his trust in the Lord and pressed on and completed his next assignment.

• Fear of Embarrassment. This fear is clearly pride. In fact the writer to the Hebrews refers to it as the sin which so easily besets us. Pride is the real reason for our unwillingness to attempt things. Even people who are overly shy suffer from an ironic twist of pride. An inferiority complex is also linked to pride.

Do you know what lies at the root of embarrassment? What situations embarrass you? I decided to do a little primary research and ask some of our staff what embarrasses them. Here is a list I received from my secretary, my daughter, our computer programmer and marriage counselor, and my teenage son and his friend:

When people make fun of me.
When I find out I was wrong after I stated I was right.
When people get the best of me.
When I am clumsy or do something awkward.
When I am really serious about something and people treat it lightly.
When people compliment me.

Most of us can identify with these sources of embarrassment. The root of the problem? Self-centered pride. The more obvious manifestations of pride include the haughty look, self-exaltation, and arrogance. But the subtlety of humble pride is just as destructive and will lead to the same doom.

Whenever we fail to make decisions because of their potential for embarrassment, we are languishing in pride which will swallow the potential God intends for our lives. The sin of pride will polarize our behavior. It will result in arrogance or silence, and either one will rob us of accomplishment.

Courage
"Then Jonathan said to the young man who was carrying his armor, 'Come and let us cross over to the garrison of these uncircumcised; perhaps the Lord will work for us, for the Lord is not restrained to save by many or by few'" (1 Samuel 14:6).

The context of this verse is one of the most exciting stories in the Bible. The Children of Israel, led by King Saul, were preparing for war against the Philistines, when there developed a few problems. The Israelites started with an army of 3,000 which dwindled to a mere 600. Also, because there was no blacksmith in the country, they had no weapons.

They were going to fight the Philistines who were only able to muster up a light force of 30,000 chariots, 6,000 horsemen, and foot soldiers numbering like the sand on the seashore. That was quite an army under any conditions, and more than adequate to face a mere 600—the other 2,400 were hiding in caves and forests. No wonder the Israelites were afraid.

But Prince Jonathan was persuaded that God would deliver the Israelites even under these impossible circumstances if they would put their trust in Him. So Jonathan asked his servant to help him destroy the Philistines. It was bad enough when he was with the 600, but now Jonathan was being outright foolish. At least, that is what Satan would want us to believe. The devil does not want us to apply the fact that one plus God is a majority. There is no situation too big or too small for our God.

With his servant's help, Jonathan destroyed a small garrison of Philistines. This created havoc and commotion, and then God performed a miracle and delivered Israel once again. But it took the courage of Jonathan to step out and decide that victory was already claimed. His armor bearer never questioned whether this was the thing to do. He took the vision of victory that Jonathan portrayed and followed him with calm assurance.

Winston Churchill created the same vision of victory for the British people. During the blackest moment of World War II, when France had fallen and all of Europe was under the Nazi terror and the V-2 rockets were reaching London, Winston Churchill inspired the world with these words:

We shall not flag or fail. We shall fight in France,
we shall fight on the seas and oceans, we shall fight

with growing confidence and growing strength in the air,
we shall defend our island, whatever the cost may be,
we shall fight on the beaches. . . . on the landing grounds,
we shall fight in the fields and in the streets,
we shall fight in the hills;
we shall never surrender.
(Speech in the House of Commons, June 4, 1940)

Let us therefore brace ourselves to our duties,
and so bear ourselves that, if the British Empire
and its Commonwealth last for a thousand years,
men will still say: "This was their finest hour."
(Speech in the House of Commons, June 18, 1940)

It takes courage to apply blind faith and trust in God. It takes courage to be willing to face consequences. It requires courage to resist the pressure of peers. It requires courage to set goals and work diligently until they are accomplished. It takes courage, not to allow others to push you off track. It takes courage to be willing to fail, and then to pick yourself up and keep on going. It requires courage to look beyond the present problems and visualize victory.

Life calls for courage, and success belongs to those who can say with the courage of Joshua, "Choose for yourselves today whom you will serve . . . as for me and my house, we will serve the Lord" (Joshua 24:15).

6

Characteristics of a Healthy Self-Image—II

His day began like a dozen others. When it ended, this navy flier began four years of psychological terror. His plane was shot down that day. When he parachuted to the ground, he was met by the Viet Cong who were freely roaming the jungles of South Vietnam. After a period of severe interrogation, he was imprisoned in a box. The box that would be his home for the next four years was a tiger cage, four and one-half feet long, three feet high, and three feet wide. Made of bamboo poles tied together with jungle vine, the cage was a mobile prison. When the Viet Cong needed to move, they simply carried him on their shoulders.

Can you begin to imagine what that would be like? Besides the obvious inconveniences and the terror, he didn't understand one word of their language. Yet he never lost sight of who he was and what his duty was. He never forgot that he was a flier for the United States Navy and that his objective was to escape, if possible. So each night when his captors were not looking, he checked every bar, examined every knot, and pushed every corner.

Then came that unbelievable moment when he pushed against a bar and found it loose. He was so excited that the adrenaline rushed through his body until he couldn't even see for a few moments. Then, as if to verify the impossible, he pushed once more and saw that the vine had rotted and the corner could easily be opened. He waited until the guards were asleep. They no longer believed that he had even the will to escape, so they left him unguarded. He pressed gently against the bamboo, being careful not to crack it, and in a few seconds squeezed his frail frame through the gap. He was delirious with excitement but observed every caution as he stole away into the darkness of the jungle. A few days later he made his way to a U.S. base—free at last!

It would be impossible to record in words the emotion he must have felt. What a thrill to realize that he did not allow the agony of isolation or the overwhelming odds of the situation to make him give up. During his imprisonment, he did what he could. He did all that he could! He checked every bar, every corner, every knot—every night!

That is exactly what these 12 characteristics of a healthy self-image are all about. You need to be measuring yourself, checking each situation in your life that may be keeping you imprisoned in a poor self-image. God intended you to use the gifts He has given you to the fullest. To do otherwise is to deny the power of the Gospel and your responsibility to the Lord.

The Parable of the Talents as told in Matthew 25 clearly describes this responsibility. You are to faithfully exercise your talents so that you may grow. The Lord honored those who multiplied their talents. But He dealt very harshly with the one who timorously hid the talent, afraid to lose it. There is an expression which illustrates the principle behind this parable—use it or lose it.

Let us take a look at seven more characteristics of people with a strong and healthy biblically based self-image:

Humilty
"Pride goes before destruction, and a haughty spirit before stumbling" (Proverbs 16:18).

Have you ever wondered why pride and a haughty spirit usher in failure? I can think of at least two reasons.

First, a person who carries the arrogance of pride in his speech and behavior generates in other people a desire to see him fall. Now while that may not sound very spiritual, it is the real world.

A second reason is that a person who is proud begins to believe himself invincible. Rather than continuing to fortify his position, he becomes careless and neglects to look after the little things. You have seen that same thing in sports—teams or athletes feeling so confident that they fail to train like they should. And destruction strikes like a thunderbolt.

Vince Lombardi, the coaching legend of the Green Bay Packers, would not allow his team to relax in victory or take anything for granted. A friend of mine, Paul Bourguinon, was a close friend of Lombardi. Having worked with Vince for a number of years, Paul was able to tell me many stories.

Coach Lombardi was a fierce competitor. But the real battle, to his way of thinking, was practice. The game was merely a reflection of the attitude and determination the team showed during the week. He was bullheaded about little things. He stressed fundamentals and knew that the team which perfected them always won in the long run. As if to underline this, he began every practice by holding a football high in the air and announcing to the team, "This is a football." Now that's really what you call a fundamental.

A humorous story is told of Max McGee, the team's practical joker, during his first practice. Vince had just completed the ceremony of announcing, "This is a football" when Max impatiently interrupted, "Hold it, Coach. You're going too fast." That outburst cost him dearly because Lombardi was deadly serious about little things. He knew that even professionals had better not forget the basics.

Solomon shares a deep truth in his Song. "Take us the foxes, the little foxes, that spoil the vines" (2:15, KJV). We must always watch out for the "little foxes" which can steal a fruitful life from us.

Little things keep relationships together. It is not the extravagant gift a wife longs for, but rather the little acts of tenderness.

If you will but look after the little foxes—your attitudes and your willingness to be humble—God will bless you with a truly abundant life. Exalt yourself and you will not come near Him. Humble yourself and He will come to you.

Humor

"A time to weep, and a time to laugh" (Ecclesiastes 3:4, KJV).

One who has a strong and healthy self-image has the capacity to laugh, even at himself. Or perhaps that should be—especially at himself. It takes a great inner strength to find humor in our own mistakes.

Duffy Dougherty, the former head football coach at Michigan State, always spotted three qualities in his exceptional football players. He looked for wishbone (that's vision), backbone (that's courage), and funnybone (that's humor).

Winston Churchill had a sense of humor that kept him from being knocked off track. Many people tried to annoy or ridicule him, but he never let this phase him one bit. George Bernard Shaw, the playwright, who was never at a loss for words, sent Churchill the following invitation:

Dear Mr. Prime Minister,
Please accept these two tickets to the opening show of my new play next Friday evening. I understand your wife is visiting in Europe. So please bring a friend, if you can find one.   Shaw

Sir Winston turned the invitation over and responded:

Dear Shaw,
I am terribly sorry I can't attend your opening performance on Friday next. Please send me two tickets for Saturday night, if the play is still running.   Churchill

When our family moved to Canada we settled in the Royal City of Guelph, Ontario, where the New York Rangers operated a junior farm team. I recall the indomitable Eddie Shack. When Eddie arrived in Guelph from northern Ontario, rumor had it that he couldn't sign his name to the contract. Though he went on to be a star hockey player with the New York Rangers and the Toronto Maple Leafs, he lived under the shadow of his poor education for a long time.

One night when the Rangers were playing in Detroit, Jack Adams, the General Manager for the Red Wings, kept yelling, "Hey, Shack, you're a real dummy. You can't even spell your own name."

Eddie got tired of that kind of talk. Finally, he made a fantastic move on a defenseman and went in and scored a super goal. Immediately, he skated over to the Detroit bench and, as only Shack could do, yelled, "Hey, Adams, that's a goal—G-O-A-L!" Then he laughed and skated back to his bench.

There is a time to weep and a time to laugh. The time to laugh and feel good about yourself is when you have done your very best. The time to weep is when you haven't.

Teachability

"A wise man will hear and increase in learning, and a man of understanding will acquire wise counsel.... Fools despise wisdom and instruction" (Proverbs 1:5, 7).

Have you ever known someone who has already learned everything you are sharing? I can think of one man like that. Every time we are in conversation and I am talking about some new idea or concept, he develops this silly, "Yeah, I know all about it" grin on his face. How do you think I feel at that moment? If I wanted to hyperspiritualize, I would tell you that he didn't affect me one bit. But you know and I know that I would be lying.

This man is basically insecure. He is uncomfortable with anyone expressing a new idea that might make him appear inferior. A person with a healthy self-image is not intimidated by new ideas. Rather, he is stimulated into new areas of thought and growth.

When General Douglas MacArthur was asked what made him a great five star general, he replied, "By being an obedient, observant first lieutenant." He knew that his growth was dependent on how well he listened and learned from others. That did not mean that he followed all the advice he was given. Certainly not. But he did not rob himself of the input necessary to make a wise decision. His men respected him for the passion he had for their input.

Proverbs 1:5 says, "A wise man will hear." Romans 10:17 says, "Faith comes from hearing." It seems that hearing unlocks the door to our understanding. The hearing referred to includes our emotional, psychological, and cultural perceptions.

One of the greatest problems a teacher or pastor has is to ensure that people are actually listening. For if they are not listening, they are not hearing. Here are a few common barriers to effective listening:

- Viewing the topic as uninteresting.
- Criticizing the delivery of the topic.
- Overstimulation about a certain point.
- Trying to find weaknesses or errors.
- Faking attention.
- Concentrating on emotion-laden words or concepts
- Permitting personal prejudice or deep-seated convictions to impair comprehension.

When the Apostle Paul outlined for Timothy the qualities and spiritual characteristics essential for church leadership, he included the ability to teach. "An overseer, then must be above reproach, the husband of one wife, temperate, prudent, respectable, hospitable, able to teach" (1 Timothy 3:2). When writing to Titus, Paul spoke of a leader this way: "Holding fast the faithful Word as he hath been taught" (1:9, KJV). Paul was not only declaring that an elder should be able to teach, but that he should be teachable, so that he might be able to encourage others with the sound doctrine he had been taught.

People who have a strong self-image are excited about

learning new ideas and new concepts, for these enable them to live more effectively.

Perseverance

"Tribulation brings about perseverance; and perseverance, proven character; and proven character, hope" (Romans 5:3-4).

Thomas Carlyle had just completed a 1,000-page handwritten manuscript on the history of the French Revolution. He had researched meticulously. He had studied diligently. He had written faithfully. And he was delighted with the finished product. He took it to his next-door neighbor, John Stuart Mill, the brilliant philosopher. Carlyle wanted Mill to read and critically evaluate the book before he took it to a publisher.

After a few days Carlyle wondered if Mill had finished reading it yet. A week passed, and then two. Carlyle really wondered what had happened. He began to think that maybe Mill didn't like the work and couldn't think how to tell him.

A few days later Mill knocked at the door and sheepishly looked at Carlyle. He told how he had read the book a few days after he received it, and then had left it on the mantle above the fireplace. His maid came in the next morning and used the manuscript pages to light the fire. Carlyle became quite emotional as he realized that several years of research and writing had literally gone up in smoke.

Carlyle remained depressed for several weeks, determined never to write again. He had the classic and understandable self-pity syndrome. However, one day as Carlyle was out walking, he noticed a mason building a very long and high wall. He observed him for several days as he labored alone, faithfully laying brick after brick.

Then one day as Carlyle watched, he became inspired with the simple notion that this long, high wall could only be built one brick at a time. One brick at a time! This thought inspired him to rewrite the book. He knew that as long as he kept this thought before him he would accomplish his goal. Carlyle proceeded to write a book which has stood the test of time as the finest history of the French Revolution.

Most people are impatient because they live in the bondage of demanding perfection. Perfectionists are always dissatisfied. When will we ever recognize that we are imperfect people living in an imperfect world? Patient people live with and even tolerate imperfection. In fact, imperfection is a stimulant to excellence. A patient man will always strive for excellence. That is character, and where there is character there is hope. No matter how dark a situation may appear, if you have the character which has been produced through patience and tribulation, you will overcome.

Friendship
"A man that hath friends must show himself friendly" (Proverbs 18:24, KJV).

I shall never forget the night that Billy McCallum died. He was a very close friend of the family, and especially of my dad. In fact, we knew him when we all lived in Belfast. Billy had been suffering for some time but he was relatively young, still in his early 60s. He had had several heart attacks and each one took its toll.

That evening, we received a phone call from Billy's wife, Florence, to run over to the hospital. My father had spent the day with us at our home. He did this quite often after Mother died. As we left for the hospital together, he was in deep thought, no doubt searching for words to share and asking the Lord to use him to comfort Billy's family.

When we arrived in the dimly lit room, Billy's family were around his bed talking quietly. When Billy heard Dad's voice, he seemed to gain extra strength and beckoned him to his side. Those next moments I will never forget, for this was certainly the most precious conversation between these old friends I have ever listened in on. Billy told Dad that he knew he was about to enter into glory. He thanked Dad for the love and friendship they had had for each other over the years. Dad told him that he didn't think he would be too far behind. Then just as naturally as if they were talking about next week's Sunday services, Dad asked Billy to be sure to say hello to my mom, and to others who had gone on before. Billy smiled and said he would. Then he added, "Sam, I'll be in the reception line when you come home."

The conversation ended as these two old friends embraced and said their good-byes. We left the family to their final farewells and headed for home. Billy was gone within an hour.

What a beautiful experience to have shared. I have often thanked the Lord for it and have longed for that quiet, natural relationship with other people and with the Lord. The friendship between Billy and my dad was the result of a love and tenderness that only the Lord can give. Such friendship is measured by our ability and willingness to give.

There are many lonely people in the world, but their loneliness may be a result of an unwillingness to give. Sometimes it is due to an unwillingness to forgive. Or an unwillingness to love. Or to tolerate, to endure, to live in peace, to be patient, to show self-control.

If people don't know why they are without friends, they should begin by asking, "Do I show myself friendly? Is the fruit of the Spirit evident in my life?" One who has a strong and healthy, biblically based self-image is usually recognized by others as friendly.

Gentleness

"Thou hast given me the shield of Thy salvation; Thy right hand sustains me, Thy gentleness has made me great" (Psalm 18:35, BERK).

Do you know anyone who has a fetish for frankness? Who is obsessed by "telling it like it is"? I have an acquaintance like that. He simply says, "That's the way I am." As if that gives him license to go around ventilating his emotions at will.

Our society has begun worshiping the macho image. Teenagers are developing an entirely new language. Just the other day I heard a young fellow referring to an automobile as a "bad car." Doesn't it seem peculiar that *bad* means *good* or that *tough* means *strong?* The new language of young people has lost a gentleness which has been replaced by a macho mania.

There is a tendency to mistake meekness for weakness. As Christians, we are admonished to be both meek and strong. There must be strength in meekness, for meekness and gentleness go hand in hand with self-control. It requires discipline and strength to refrain from "telling it like it is," to exhibit patience, waiting for the right moment to articulate the thought effectively and gently.

Sometimes Christians feel led to share an area of weakness with another brother or sister. This is biblical and is required in order to mature us as saints. But we need to look at the text wherein we find our authority. "Brethren, even if a man is caught in any trespass, you who are spiritual, restore such a one in a spirit of gentleness" (Galatians 6:1).

The goal is not to ventilate our emotions or condemn others, but to restore the fallen one. If we see this from the beginning, all of our actions will focus on how we do it—"in the spirit of meekness," gently and tenderly. When we seek retribution rather than restoration, we rob the Holy Spirit of an opportunity.

There is an expression that describes much of current church discipline—"Only evangelicals kill their wounded." Remember, truth used as a club will always drive people to error. May God help us to be firm and gentle.

Inspirational Power

"We are afflicted in every way, but not crushed; perplexed, but not despairing; persecuted, but not forsaken; struck down, but not destroyed" (2 Corinthians 4:8-9).

Could there ever be more inspiring words than these? They came from one who had suffered intensely but who never gave up. The Apostle Paul had known many setbacks, yet he endured and became an inspiration to every Christian worker, indeed to everyone who will ever face difficulty and tribulation. Look at some of the setbacks Paul encountered from his first missionary journey, recorded in Acts 13—15.

● Opposition. While on Cyprus he contended with Elymas the sorcerer.

● Sickness. Paul got malaria at Pamphylia and had to go to the mountains.

● Hostile environment. The regions north of Pamphylia were filled with robbers and murderers who preyed on lonely travelers.

● Desertion. John Mark, Barnabas' cousin, decided to go home rather than stay with Paul and Barnabas.

● Persecution. This setback followed them everywhere from Pisidian Antioch, Iconium, Lystra, and Derbe.

● Flattery. Satan's insidious plot to prey on every man's weakness befell Paul and Barnabas at Lystra. The people there thought the two men were gods and treated them royally. What a temptation!

● Doctrinal error. After being gone for three long, hard years, how disappointing it must have been for these missionaries to find a group of "believing" Pharisees corrupting the truth of the Gospel by telling new Christians that they must also obey the ceremonial laws of Moses.

● Personal disappointment. Paul and Barnabas argued about whether John Mark should accompany them on the second missionary journey. Barnabas wanted to encourage Mark, but Paul wanted to have a courageous, united team. Both were right and both were wrong. They were certainly disappointed in each other, but they didn't let that deter them. Barnabas took Mark and went to Cyprus; Paul chose Silas and left for Galatia and parts unknown.

Even after all this the Apostle Paul still kept his eyes on Jesus. He pressed on and on, into Satan's territory, confident that Christ would sustain him and be glorified in his weakness.

Inspirational power emanates from those who have tenaciously fought off problems to achieve their goals. One who has this charisma readily projects trust and confidence. Many people long for others to admire them. This is only natural. But it is more than natural if you can be entrusted with heavy responsibility and yet not think of yourself more highly than you ought. The power to do this does not come from holding tightly but from keeping an open hand—allowing the Holy Spirit to have full sway in every area of your life.

David was accused by his brothers of pride and arrogance when he declared that he would fight Goliath. David probably did sound a bit brash when he said to King Saul, "Don't let any of your warriors be afraid any longer. I'll go and put an end to this Philistine."(See 1 Samuel 17:32.)

Have you ever wondered about the fine line between honest confidence and arrogant pride? Are we not instructed to do everything to the best of our ability? Are we not to believe that with God all things are possible? We must be careful not to quench the spirit of a person who is naive enough to come as a little child and believe. We must be careful not to engrave our doubts, our lack of faith, and our fears on the hearts of our friends and family. Can you imagine how David's faith increased that day?

Perhaps if David had not faced Goliath he would never have been able to write Psalm 27 which begins:

The Lord is my light and my salvation;
whom shall I fear?
The Lord is the strength of my life;
of whom shall I be afraid? (KJV)

7

In
Search of
Blind Spots—I

"Faithful are the wounds of a friend; but deceitful are the kisses of an enemy" (Proverbs 27:6).

Last year our family took a brief vacation in Tampa, Florida. Since Brenda was spending her summer in the jungles of Peru, we borrowed an economy car that we thought would be big enough for six people. As it turned out, we were crammed in like toothpicks in a jar, and the "easy" trip to Tampa felt like a 30-hour ride to Toronto.

To make matters worse, I couldn't see out of the rearview mirror without asking the children to move their heads. It was impossible to get them to do so in unison. As a result, I was dependent on Brent to tell me when it was safe to turn or to move back into the nonpassing lane.

Brent could see it was difficult for me to rely on his directions. So he said, "Dad, you have to believe me. This is a real lesson in trust." So true. He was my eyes. He was able to fill in my blind spots, because he could see things from a better perspective.

In a similar way, our family and friends often see things in our lives from a clearer perspective. We all have emotional blind spots we cannot see. Sometimes we become aware of our blind spots because we see them in the lives of others, and then can recognize them in ourselves.

Such was the case with the Prophet Nathan and King David. It seems impossible to believe that David needed to hear Nathan's parable to realize the depravity of his own heart. How could anyone deliberately send another to his death? Yet that is precisely what David had done to Uriah, when he took Bathsheba, Uriah's wife.

Nathan used a third-party illustration to gain David's attention and also to avoid his emotional blind spot. Nathan related a parable of a rich man who had many sheep and of a poor man who had only one. When Nathan told David that the rich man stole the poor man's only lamb, David became angry, declaring that the man who had done this thing would surely die. (See 2 Samuel 12.)

Then in a climax of emotion Nathan pointed his finger at the king and said, "Thou art the man." David recognized his sin and repented. It took courage for Nathan to confront the powerful king. But God loved David and could not condone his behavior. David softened in the face of this clear revelation.

In this chapter and the two which follow, we will deal with specific behaviors in a manner similar to Nathan's parable. In each case a question will be asked which highlights a particular behavior. The question is in order to encourage you to become introspective. The illustrations and Scripture accompanying each question should provide a clear perspective, so that you can confront issues in your life.

Are You Consistent?

"A double-minded man is unstable in all his ways" (James 1:8, KJV).

Years ago when we lived in Guelph, Ontario, an incident took place that taught me much about the bad habit of inconsistency.

One morning I was rushing home, having just dropped off some of our children at school. Bradley, our youngest, was not yet in school, and was standing on the backseat leaning over my shoulder as I drove. My mind was on something else, but I do remember racing down a hill on a four-lane road, anxious to get home. Then Bradley taught me a lesson which has made an indelible impression on me to this day.

He said, "Dad, you're going 50 miles an hour." The first thing I thought was, "How does he know that?" I didn't think he could understand a speedometer. Feeling guilty, but trying not to show it, I asked rather indignantly, "So what?" To which he replied, "But the speed limit is 30."

I was amazed that he knew all about miles per hour and speed limits. But his remarks also revealed something to me about my nature. I discovered that I thought it was perhaps all right to do something wrong, as long as I was not caught. I would never before have admitted to such a thought.

I learned yet another truth—that I was teaching my children a double standard. I certainly was not doing so deliberately, but the results could be just as damaging. I was teaching them to say one thing and do another. I was giving them a vivid illustration that talk did not have to be congruent with actions. In other words, "Do as I say, not as I do!"

Right about that time, I had been giving a lot of thought to problems certain parents were having with their teenagers. They were perplexed at the rebellion in their homes. I knew these people and was confident that they didn't expect such problems. As I asked why it happened to them, I kept remembering my own double standard.

For most adults, driving above the speed limit is no big problem. But to a young child in the socialization process, exceeding the speed limit is breaking the law and therefore wrong. While in the developmental stage of life, young children are being molded to believe that a double standard in life is perfectly acceptable.

Are you consistent? It requires discipline to stand for principles. It requires inner strength to make sure that what you say is what you do. A person's real character comes out in what he does when no one is watching.

Are You Self-Controlled?

"Moreover we know that to those who love God, who are called according to His plan, everything that happens fits into a pattern for good" (Romans 8:28, PH).

This verse does not say that everything that happens is good. But rather that everything will turn out for good. The evidence of our walk in the Spirit is the fruit of the Spirit, which includes the quality of self-control or temperance. Have you ever asked yourself why it is a mark of distinction to manifest a controlled life? What is meant by self-control? When is self-control taken to the extreme?

The self-control referred to in Scripture is the quality of abiding or resting in the Lord. When the world is being torn apart, when tensions and trials persist, when men's hearts are failing them, the Spirit of God enables believers to demonstrate a peace and tranquillity which surpass all understanding. The family of God knows that even what men might intend for evil, God will turn to good. God will use every circumstance of our lives to perfect us and make us more like His dear Son.

One reason a spiritual leader must exhibit the fruit of self-control is to preserve stability. People are looking for reality—and they have it in the pressures of everyday living:

- The reality of job insecurity.
- The reality of family problems.
- The reality of financial difficulty.
- The reality of church problems.
- The reality of feeling inadequate.
- The reality of the future.
- The reality of the past.

These pressures are common to all of us. But those who desire to be leaders of men must learn how to react in crisis. The true measure of a leader is not what he does when all is going as planned, but what he does in the storm. When he suddenly discovers that a catastrophe has occurred. When he learns that he didn't get the job, couldn't buy that house, couldn't go away on vacation. When he has a business collapse, when his friends forsake him.

For handling such problems, Jesus says, "Cast all your cares on Me for I care for you." and "Come to Me all of you who are weary and overburdened and I will give you rest." (See 1 Peter 5:7 and Matthew 11:28-30.) In the turbulence, it is our responsibility to exhibit self-control, not only to help ourselves but also those around us.

Several years ago I had a speaking engagement in the Ontario city of Sudbury, and was flying there with an associate from Toronto, John Garnett. John was well aware that I was a "white-knuckle" flyer. I have changed somewhat over the years, but flying is not my favorite means of travel.

The first leg of the flight took us to North Bay. John hadn't told me how we were to fly from North Bay to Sudbury. After a layover of a few hours, John led me through a door and out onto the runway. I was flabbergasted—all I could see was a tiny, twin-engine aircraft that John seemed determined was for us. I told him there was no way I was going in that plane. We discussed it at some length and he assured me this was our only alternative.

Very reluctantly, I boarded Bradley Airlines. I thought, "How ridiculous! John and I are the only passengers in this six-seater and there are two pilots." We took off shortly after dark, for my first flight on a small plane.

As the plane rumbled and roared down the runway, I could feel every bump. The engines got louder and louder and I thought we would never be airborne. We wavered in the air, gained altitude, and rattled indiscriminately. Needless to say, I was undergoing great discomfort.

A forest fire along the shores of Lake Nipissing was drawing the attention of both the pilots and John. They were staring intently out of the windows on the left side of the plane. I was seated behind the copilot, beside the engine which was mounted on the right wing. As we were climbing, my eyes were fixed straight ahead until a blue flame suddenly shot out from the right engine. It was one of those moments when you feel like telling someone what you saw, yet you don't want to appear foolish or afraid. So I kept quiet. Then a few moments later another blue flame shot out and I decided that John should enjoy the experience with me. His eyes seemed to rotate in their sockets—he was so scared.

When the pilot saw the flame, he cut off the fuel supply to the engine. Immediately the torque caused the plane to perform a sweeping "Sky King" maneuver. We lost altitude and raced toward the treetops. I have never been more terrified.

The main reason for my horror was not the fact that I was flying in a small plane or even that the engine was on fire. I was most horrified by the look of terror on the face of the pilot when he saw the flames. He communicated more fear to me than the actual experience. Had he kept his cool, had he remained calm, had he exhibited a strength of self-control, I would have felt a greater measure of trust and confidence. I knew the events were hazardous. I was aware of the potential for tragedy. In that crisis, I was looking to the leader for strength, stability, and assurance.

As Christians we need to overwhelm an unbelieving world with the calm, tranquil peace that only the Holy Spirit can give. We need to live above our circumstances when things go wrong. We need to be lights to those who are adrift on the raging seas of life. They should be able to recognize the control that comes from understanding that "everything that happens to God's children fits into a pattern for good."

Do You Think Independently?

"How blessed is the man who does not walk in the counsel of the wicked, nor stand in the path of sinners, nor sit in the seat of scoffers!" (Psalm 1:1)

In describing whether an individual readily conforms to the pressure of a group or resists such pressure, psychologists refer to the person as having an internal or external locus of control. In other words, the place or the locus which motivates behavior is either from his inner personal convictions or from the external mores of his peer group.

An individual with a strong and healthy self-image is more

capable of resisting peer pressure when the group is engaging in behavior contrary to his personal convictions or desires. This in no way infers that he is an outcast to the group. In fact, quite the contrary. The person who has the inner strength to say no when he senses the need is often the one seen by the group as a potential leader. However, group members will eventually resist his leadership if it violates their desires too often.

At the critical moment of decision, the choice for the leader is tough. The ultimate question is, "What is more important to me, the glory of the group or my personal convictions?"

Everyone recognizes the classic conformist— the person who sticks his finger in the air to see which way the group is going. He simply follows the group. Psychologists refer to this person as a group dependent.

On the other hand, the classic nonconformist is an arrogant, inflexible, immature buffoon. He sticks his finger in the air to see which way the group is going so that he can go the other way. He is just as group-dependent as the conformist, for he needs the group to tell him which way not to go.

Conformists and nonconformists have a lot in common. They do not reason for themselves. They do not judge for themselves. They do not apply values for themselves. They do not test situations for themselves. They have abdicated their responsibilities to others. What a shame!

I had a professor in graduate school who taught me a great lesson in this regard. One day after class he asked me to come with him to his office.

He sat quietly for a few moments just staring at me. Then he said, "Cliff, it's really too bad. "You have a convoy mentality! Don't waste your life by constantly following the decisions of others." At first I was puzzled until I recalled that a convoy is a naval term which refers to a series of ships that follow one after the other. My professor was certainly not suggesting that I was the flagship.

I left his office with a new lease on life. He had confronted me with my behavior, and I had no great difficulty in recognizing the problem. I became aware of times I followed the influence of others. For a while I almost went overboard on the other side, until I realized that while advice from others was vital, I didn't need to feel pressured to follow it.

Psalm 1:1 is a perfect portrayal of those who are externally controlled. Even though young people have been raised in homes with Christian principles and values, they can easily succumb to the pressures of the world if they allow themselves to be tantalized by people in the world.

Notice that there are three action words—walk, stand, and sit— which show the move away from godly involvement. It begins by walking close to the things of the world. This most often happens by simple associations at school or in business. Certainly we are a part of the world and cannot, and indeed ought not, be isolated from it. But the indication by the psalmist here is that the walking is a deliberate choice to be with the ungodly when it is not necessary.

Once we have broken the first barrier it is easier to feel comfortable standing with them. Standing denotes an attitude of accepting or at least condoning their values. This standing is a deliberate choice of the will. The behavior finally results in worldly involvement when we sit down to relax and engage as full members of the group.

What God wants for His children is independence from the influence of all that does not glorify Him. He wants and demands an absolute dependence on Himself.

Can You Handle Negative Criticism?
"Let us not lose heart in doing good, for in due time we shall reap if we do not grow weary" (Galatians 6:9).

As the Prime Minister of Great Britain during World War II, Winston Churchill spent many wearisome days. Parliament would be in session late each day, and he would then have to consult with his cabinet and chiefs of staff in the War Room. Like any great leader, he knew that it was impossible to please everyone. Indeed, there are those who never will be satisfied. Such was Lady Astor.

According to Sir Winston, Lady Astor spent much of her time looking for issues on which to confront and embarrass him. He always had the last say and Lady Astor always went away frustrated. One day in an effort to display disgust and outrage at one of Sir Winston's decisions, Lady Astor stood and hollered across the floor of Parliament: "Sir Winston, if I were your wife, I would poison your tea." Churchill rose to his feet, and politely replied, "Lady Astor, let me assure you, if I were your husband, I would drink it." While I am not suggesting we resort to scathing sarcasm, this story does illustrate the need to maintain our direction when we know it to be right.

Through all the criticism and physical suffering which the Apostle Paul endured, he never let his vision be blurred. He remained totally unmoved. In his second letter to his son in the faith, Timothy, Paul encouraged and motivated with these words: "You, however, continue in the things you have learned and become convinced of, knowing from whom you have learned them" (2 Timothy 3:14).

It is difficult to discriminate between constructive, biblical criticism which is for our good, and destructive, negative criticism which is of the devil and designed to push us off track. How do we recognize the difference? Here are some suggestions:

• What was the attitude of the one delivering the criticism? Was the criticism given in a spirit of meekness, with a desire for restoration and growth? Or was it given in a haughty spirit?

• Regardless of the attitude of the one who was criticizing, was the message such that you know in your heart it is true? If so, accept it as from the Lord and correct your life accordingly.

• Even if you cannot readily accept the truth of the message, allow the Holy Spirit to search your blind spots for areas you have never seen before.

• Take time to speak to someone you trust, and share the criticism. Encourage that friend to be faithful to you to verify or negate the criticism.

• Once you have dealt with the criticism, ask God to free you from the potential condemnation of its message.

Do You Use Disappointments Creatively?

"Now when I came to Troas for the Gospel of Christ and when a door was opened for me in the Lord, I had no rest for my spirit, not finding Titus my brother; but taking my leave of them, I went on to Macedonia. But thanks be to God, who always leads us in His triumph in Christ, and manifests through us the sweet aroma of the knowledge of Him in every place" (2 Corinthians 2:12-14).

Clearly Paul was disappointed. Titus missed his meeting with him, and this created tension. Paul could have floundered. He could have felt sorry for himself and wondered if anyone else cared. The disappointment might have caused Paul to reorient his vision and his purpose. Instead, he declared how wonderful God is for always leading us along a triumphant path.

Seeing God's hand in his disappointment, Paul set his sights across the Aegean Sea to the shores of Macedonia. I often wonder how many opportunities for service we miss because we fail to use our disappointments creatively.

Several years ago I was conducting a sales management seminar for a large real estate firm in Chicago. We were engaged in a brainstorming session dealing with factors which cause salespeople to burnout and leave the industry. One factor is the way a person handles disappointments. This is certainly not isolated to the real estate industry.

One of the greatest disappointments to a real estate sales-person is to lose a potential buyer in whom he has invested a great deal of time. He may have neglected to contact the buyer for a few days and then discovers that the client has purchased from someone else. It is hard for the salesperson to understand, and generally his reaction is anger. Sometimes the anger is at himself, but most often it is directed at the client.

I worked in real estate for several years, and can recall salespeople telephoning clients and expressing their emotions with a measure of hostility. If they didn't call, they at least tore the prospect card into a dozen pieces and never contacted the client again.

At this particular seminar, a very successful manager shared an idea that showed how to use a disappointment creatively. Rather than throwing away a prospect card, he filed it for future use, just as though he had sold the home. After a few days, he sat down and wrote the former prospect a letter, telling them how much he appreciated the opportunity to serve them, and expressing how pleased he was they had found the home they desired. He wished them many happy and successful years, and said if they needed help for anything in the future, they were simply to call him. He also sent them a card on the anniversary date of the house purchase.

You can see the tremendous impact this would have. Jack kept records. Of those who sold those homes within a few years, he got over 80 percent of the listings. And he could not begin to calculate the number of referrals for other buyers and sellers he received from them. What a successful way to creatively use disappointment!

8

In
Search of
Blind Spots—II

"They profess to know God, but by their deeds they deny Him, being detestable and disobedient, and worthless for any good deed" (Titus 1:16).

As a pastor it is very difficult for me to turn away anyone who needs help. Our church is on a main highway in the city of Longwood, just north of Orlando. In 1982, we had a regular flow of folks who were really down and out and in extreme need of the basics of life.

Malcolm showed up one Friday evening during a seminar. Of all the choices of seats he could have made, Malcolm sat down right beside my wife and immediately asked for the pastor. Donna nudged me and Malcolm leaned over to talk. As his volume increased I realized we had better go outside.

Malcolm had arrived in town a week or so before, and neither he nor his wife had eaten much for a few days. His employer had not been honorable about paying him, and he had no money. He did not ask me for money, but wanted to know if he could do some work around the church in return for food or money. This impressed me and I was anxious that we do what we could.

Later, the chairman of our deacon board, Bob Heroy,

came into my office and we talked about Malcolm. Both of us really felt led to let him work on the duplex we were cleaning for one of our missionary families. So he was scheduled to work the next day from 8 A.M. to 6 P.M. for which he would earn $50. That evening we gave him a gift of $20 for some food.

Well, the next day he showed at 10 A.M. and left at 3 P.M. The job was not done. In fact, Bob had to work with him to keep him on the job. We paid him only for the hours he worked. He came to church on Sunday, and after the services, while I was greeting people at the door, he kept interrupting me. Finally I excused myself from some folks to talk with him. He told me he had to have at least $65 more to pay for his motel room. I explained that he had been a disappointment on Saturday and that we would not be giving him anything else, since he had not shown himself faithful.

That instant, a change took place in him—his face gnarled, his voice became gruff, his body language turned hostile. I actually thought he was going to strike me. He slammed his way out the door, shouting profanities. He tore his bulletin, yelled at folks standing on the front lawn, climbed into his car and peeled out of the church lot screaming obscenities.

Truly Malcolm had a reprobate mind, with blind spots on top of blind spots. He was incapable of discerning good from evil. The greatest tragedy was that he professed to know God but denied Him in his works.

As we continue with our questions, remember that their purpose is to reveal areas of need in your life, as you work toward a strong and healthy self-image.

Do You Receive Cooperation, Respect, and Confidence?

"And his armor-bearer said to him, 'Do all that is in your heart; turn yourself, and here I am with you according to your desire'" (1 Samuel 14:7).

Jonathan had asked his armor-bearer to go with him to fight against the Philistines. Though it was definitely a suicide mission, the armor-bearer agreed. Notice the respect and confidence he bestowed upon Jonathan. What he said was, "Jonathan, I trust you, because I know you. I know you, because I have seen your heart in action. And Jonathan, if you act according to the direction of your heart, I am with you all the way. But if for one moment I think you are doing otherwise, I will lose respect and confidence and I will quit."

This is what many children are silently saying to their moms and dads—"I will respect you and have confidence in you if I see that you have integrity."

Integrity means being willing to stand up for principles, when it isn't easy to do so. Integrity means being willing to tell your children you are sorry when you have done wrong. Integrity means that you are the same person at home as you are anywhere else.

When you win the respect and confidence of others, they will usually do what you request because they trust you and want to cooperate.

Can You Discipline Without a Show of Authority?

"I will instruct you and teach you in the way which you should go; I will counsel you with My eye upon you" (Psalm 32:8).

I am the youngest of three boys. My brothers are five and ten years older. When I was small we attended a prestigious Presbyterian church in Belfast. My father was an elder and took his position very seriously.

Our family sat in a front pew to one side of the platform. We were in full view of everyone. As a result Dad wanted to be sure his family was well-behaved.

On those occasions when boys will be boys, all Dad had to do was lean forward ever so slightly, and pull his bushy eyebrows into a frown. Then he would motion with his eyes for us to sit still, be quiet, sit back, and look straight ahead. Now that was some feat, especially since it all took place in a couple of seconds. That is the picture I always see when I read Psalm 32:8.

A *position* of authority does not guarantee obedience. Obedience is the result of either fear or respect. Respect is generally the recognition that one can exercise authority and deliver punishment, if necessary. However, another course of action, such as encouragement, is preferable. Encouragement always paves the way for learning. People will more readily accept correction if it comes from one who also knows how to encourage and does so liberally.

One of the summer mission projects with which we were involved was with the Ayore Indians in Bolivia. A missionary and I were riding in a truck with Ahoi, the chief of the Ayores, who began to share some of the earlier tribal customs. He told how important it was for mothers to make sure their children were silent when the tribe was hiding in the jungle, avoiding ambush or attack from other tribes.

Think of your own actions. Do you always have to display authority to get the job done? Do you have to threaten to see your word obeyed? The key word here is always. If you always have to threaten and resort to a show of authority, you are displaying weakness rather than strength. The inner strength which calls for respect is a sign of a strong and healthy self-image. Threats and outbursts of authority are significant indicators of emotional insecurity and feelings of inferiority.

Are You a Peacemaker?

"Blessed are the peacemakers; for they shall be called the children of God" (Matthew 5:9, KJV).

To be a peacemaker is to act like a child of God. Why? Because it is so unnatural for us to want to bring peace. Our nature thrives on conflict, particularly if we are spectators to it or on the winning side.

The Apostle Peter was a tempestuous character. He was truly an "ear-cutter" who would rather fight than switch. His first reaction was to come out with guns blazing and ask questions later. I have seen many modern day Peters, haven't you?

Early in the discipling process, Peter wanted the Lord to give him some leeway for his impulsiveness. Yet he knew too that he had to show some restraint. Seeking acceptable limitations for his behavior, he asked, "Master, how many times can my brother wrong me and I must forgive him? Would seven times be enough?"

"No," replied Jesus, "not seven times, but seventy times seven!" In other words, he was to forgive and to bring peace an unlimited number of times. Whenever the natural desire for conflict emerges, we are to seek to live peaceably. (See Matthew 18:21-35.)

Most discussions which lead to arguments generate more heat than light. We seem to have a passion within us to prove we are right. It isn't good enough for us just to believe we are right. We feel the need to persuade and to browbeat others to our way of thinking.

When a discussion degenerates to emotional confrontation, someone has to stop. The one who constantly needs to have the last word is the most insecure.

Robbie Burns, the Scottish poet, recited no truer words than these: "A man convinced against his will is of the same opinion still."

Those who are emotionally strong, with a positive self-image, do not have this inordinate need to win every argument, to defeat and disprove every opinion variant to their own.

Most people will change their views when they see living proof of a better way. There is magnificent character and strength in one who shares by deed, who persuades through action, who leads by example, and who pours oil on troubled waters.

Can You Handle Difficult Situations?

"The word of the Lord came to Elijah in the third year, saying, 'Go, show yourself to Ahab, and I will send rain on the face of the earth.'

"And it came about, when Ahab saw Elijah that Ahab said

to him, 'Is this you, you troubler of Israel?' And he said, 'I have not troubled Israel, but you and your father's house have, because you have forsaken the commandments of the Lord, and you have followed the Baals'" (1 Kings 18:1, 17-18).

Certainly Elijah had his hands full. God had asked him to rebuke Ahab and tell him that there would be a drought in Israel. It was a difficult and delicate situation, but God knew that Elijah was fit for the task. God was aware that Elijah would obey Him and then go for a while to the Brook Cherith, and then on to share the food of the Zarephath widow and her son. Elijah was, so to speak, in spiritual training for the great contest on Mount Carmel.

Elijah was being prepared for his difficult situation by seeing the miraculous provision of the Lord, from the ravens at Cherith and from the poor but trusting widow at Zarephath. God had confidence that Elijah was the kind of man needed to fill the gap, and knew that he would be faithful.

If people trust you, it is because of *what* you are, not *who* you are. To be entrusted with difficult and delicate situations, you have to be willing to confront problems, share honestly, not harbor bitterness, be teachable, exercise good judgment and wisdom, be gentle and full of mercy. A spirit of humility protects you from esteeming yourself more than you ought.

Ask yourself—"Do my friends seek my counsel?" "Do my subordinates respect my advice?" "Does my family honor my decisions?" "Are my children obedient?"

Are You a Motivator?

"And walking by the Sea of Galilee, He saw two brothers, Simon who was called Peter, and Andrew his brother, casting a net into the sea; for they were fishermen. And He said to them, 'Follow Me, and I will make you fishers of men.' And they immediately left the nets, and followed Him.

"And going on from there He saw two other brothers, James the son of Zebedee, and John his brother, in the boat with Zebedee their father, mending their nets; and He called them. And they immediately left the boat and their father, and followed Him" (Matthew 4:18-22).

A person is well motivated when there is purposefulness in what he does. A person is demoralized and demotivated when he has negative, unhealthy attitudes.

Let me show you nine easy ways to demotivate your family, friends, and business associates:

• Belittle them. Not long ago, I heard a man describe his childhood. He was a brilliant student, always got straight A's. He had his Ph.D. in mathematics and had been a Rhodes scholar, but he felt unfulfilled and inferior. Why? His father never congratulated or encouraged him. If he returned from school with a 98, his father always belittled him by asking what happened to the other 2 points. He was crushed.

• Always criticize them in front of their peers. This will ensure that they will feel inferior and lack confidence to initiate anything. It will also give their peers license to ridicule and walk all over them. Certainly, if parents do not have the pride and desire to instill worth into their children, the kids will develop emotional insecurity.

Never give them your undivided attention. If you ever give people your undivided attention, they may think you are sincerely interested in them. If you want to create unhealthy attitudes, never let them believe that.

John Dreschler gives a superb illustration of this in his touching book, *If I Were to Raise My Family Again*. He tells the story of a little boy who is trying desperately to get the attention his father who is engrossed in the newspaper. The little fellow is trying to tell his daddy about falling and cutting his knee and how it hurts him so. After several such interruptions, the father impatiently and angrily scowls at the boy and asks, "What can I do about it?" The little fellow puts his head down and shuffles away saying, "You could say 'Ouch.'" How many times we forget to say "ouch" to people. How many times we are caught up in our own self-centered lives and neglect our loved ones. What a pity!

• Always appear preoccupied with your own interests. In

order to make sure that your family, friends, and work associates develop unhealthy attitudes you must not get involved in their interests. Stay busy doing your own thing. If they don't like it, too bad. Life is far too short to be involved with them. You know the attitude: "It is what I want that counts. I have to please me first. If I don't, I won't be a real person." Does that sound familiar? It's the beat of the "me" generation.

Donna and I have always felt that we should be interested in our children's activities. So Donna has arranged our schedule over the years to guarantee that we would be at such illustrious events as school musicals, picnics, volleyball games, gymnastic events, soccer tournaments, basketball games, music recitals.... It has been such fun, and the memories of all these occasions belong to us forever.

• Always play favorites. Playing favorites breeds jealousy which breeds conflict. Those who are not the favorites will never reach emotional maturity but will constantly crave attention and kindness.

Unfortunately, the fairy tale of Cinderella and the wicked stepmother who favored the older daughters is a scene playing in far too many homes. Most children pass through a phase when they feel like ugly ducklings. If they ever sense that their parents or family have rejected them, they will remain scarred for life. Therapy and surrogate love will do some good, but the scar will remain.

• Never be sensitive to small things. Sensitivity to little things in a marriage would probably let your spouse think you really cared. If you were sensitive to the little things in your children's lives, they might think you actually were concerned for them. If you want them to have demotivated, unhealthy attitudes, don't let them believe this.

One of the most frequent marriage problems I hear from both husbands and wives is, "I don't think he/she cares anymore." "Why?" I ask. I hear something like this from wives, "He doesn't surprise me with little gifts—he doesn't hug and kiss me unannounced—he doesn't look at me tenderly anymore—he is not affectionate."

Husbands are prone to say, "She is no longer interested in what I do all day—she forgets to pick up the special items for me—she is more concerned with the kids and their problems—she is not excited when I come home." Remember, it's the little foxes that kill the tender vines.

• Never let them grow. Make sure you always cast a long shadow over their lives so that they cannot reach the light. Plants don't grow strong in the shade but in sunlight. Don't allow them to mature and develop; for if they do, they will no longer be dependent on you.

When I was a professor of business at Wilfrid Laurier University in Waterloo, Ontario, one of the major reasons for dropout or failure of the third- and fourth-year students was their realization that they just didn't want to be there. Many of them had become business students under pressure from their fathers. But unfortunately, the fathers kept them in the shade and cast giant shadows. The fathers were competing with the children.

Children need the opportunity to exercise responsibility and authority over decisions within their emotional grasp. A plant will die from too much or too little food. Likewise, we should not force-feed or overfeed responsibility too early, in an effort to race our children toward adulthood. Maturity is a process, not an event.

• Always embarrass them. It is important for the development of poor attitudes to embarrass children and make them feel uncomfortable in as many situations as possible. If you make them feel awkward, they probably will not want to spend time with you, and will allow you to do what you want.

I have known many people who carry humor and fun much too far. On some occasions I have ached for the victims of their sarcasm and teasing. For I have long since learned that most sarcasm, like a political cartoon, is an abstract of reality. It does hurt and can go very deep.

• Always vascillate in decision-making. If you can keep your family on edge as far as what you are going to do, the confusion will make them insecure and uneasy. This will certainly accomplish your goal of demoralizing them and developing negative attitudes.

Isn't it appalling to think of how destructive our behaviors can be to others? Isn't it tragic to think of how many young productive minds have been scarred by insensitive behavior?

Can You Accept Disagreement Objectively?

"And He withdrew from them about a stone's throw, and He knelt down and began to pray, saying, 'Father, if Thou art willing, remove this cup from Me; yet not My will, but Thine be done'" (Luke 22:41-42).

How easily most of us are hurt and offended! How ready we are to demand our rights. I was just reading in the Orlando *Sentinel* newspaper how a six-year-old girl from Carmel, Indiana was suing the Cracker Jack Division of Borden Incorporated for neglecting to put a prize inside her box of candy-coated popcorn and peanuts.

As a sales trainer, I used to spend a great deal of time teaching trainers that when prospects reject an offer, they are rejecting the product, not the salesperson. We tend to consider all rejection as a personal affront.

My dad spent the last few years of his life as visitation pastor of our home church in Guelph, Ontario. He really thrived on getting out to meet people, morning, noon, and night. He was consumed in his ministry to reach people with the Good News of the Lord Jesus Christ. Most people could not understand how he could handle all the rejection and scoffing. He had a classic response when his message was rejected and someone scoffed at him. He said "Look, I am just delivering the royal mail. Like any mailman, I didn't write the letter. But I am responsible to deliver it."

Let's look at this from another angle. When you put your best idea forward in a meeting, and it gets knocked down, how do you react? What do you do? Do you demand your rights? Do you take your bat and ball and go home? Do you become argumentative and defensive? Do you begin to sow discord, even after a decision has been reached? What should our reaction be? You should accept difficulty as Jesus did: "Not My will but Thine be done" (Luke 22:42).

Do You Maintain Friendships?
"Give and it will be given to you" (Luke 6:38).

I heard a definition of *friend* that encapsulates the entire meaning—"A friend is someone who stays your friend after he gets to know you." The individual who stays, after all the fluff has cleared and the warts begin to show, is a true friend.

A friend does not expect perfection. A true friend realizes that we are all imperfect people living in an imperfect world. A friend knows how to say, "I'm sorry."

The concept of giving expressed in Luke 6:38 means to give according to your need. In other words, whatever you need or whatever you are really short on, that you should give. Why? Because this is a biblical formula, a law of God. Give and it will be given.

The verses just prior to this illustrate the point. To receive mercy you must give mercy. If you want to be judged, then be sure to give judgment. If you want condemnation, then you are to condemn. The principle is this: "Whatever measure you use with other people, they will use in their dealings with you."

If you want to keep friends you must give. Give what? Friendship, of course! What is friendship? Love, joy, peace, patience, kindness, generosity, fidelity, tolerance, and self-control. Sounds familiar, doesn't it?

It is so simple you could miss the profound truth of it, "Give and it will be given to you."

Do You Depend on Approval from Others?
"For they loved the approval of men rather than the approval of God" (John 12:43).

Praise is so welcome. We know how dangerous it is, yet we cannot resist it. Even when we know it is happening to us, it is so difficult to turn from it. It is like breaking our diet—we feel guilty, but it still tastes good.

The natural man craves the praise and approval of others. We are by nature people-pleasers. We need to be loved and placed on a pedestal. That has such appeal to the lusts of the flesh. In fact, it is the major reason peer pressure is such a force. You don't have to be a psychologist to know that flattery and praise are very effective tools in motivating people.

While we still lived in Ontario, our family took many vacations in the States. Often we would visit my brother Neville and his family in Illinois. On one trip something happened that showed my own vulnerability to praise.

Late one evening I got a long-distance call from Canada that necessitated our leaving Wheaton and returning home as soon as possible. We decided to leave early the next day.

Our station wagon had been packed very meticulously when we left Canada, but now we didn't take time to repack it the same way. To put it mildly, it looked like someone had thrown a grenade into it.

From years of traveling with five children, Donna and I were in the habit of last minute roll calls, making sure that the washroom had been visited, hands washed, teeth brushed, and general preparation made for the long trip. We did so that morning, but I added one thing. Brent, who is our third child and middle son, had a habit of knowing how and when to light my fire. He had already been annoying his younger brother, Bradley, and I wanted to be certain that this trip would be fairly peaceful. So I took Brent aside, and explained to him the facts of life for this road trip. I told him we needed to get home to face an emergency, and that I wanted no trouble in the third seat, since it was very difficult for me while driving 60 MPH to get his attention.

Brent was fully aware that if he caused any disturbance, he was in trouble when we stopped for gas at Benton Harbor. He assured me, "No problem, Dad, no problem."

We had not driven more than 20 minutes when I heard

the first rumblings from the rear seat. I let it go a little while but it persisted. Then I said, "Brent, I warned you. Now when we stop for gas, you and I are going to visit the washroom—together!" Instant silence.

We pulled in for gas at Benton Harbor and my mind was consumed with the situation that awaited me back in Guelph. We got back on the highway and headed for Detroit. Then it dawned on me that I had forgotten to keep my promise to Brent. I didn't want him to know that, so I looked in the rearview mirror, got his attention, and said, "I bet you think I forgot. Well, let me tell you, when we get to the border at Detroit, you and I are going to pay a visit to the washroom—together!" What a great way to discipline!

Needless to say, as we approached customs, I forgot about Brent. Every time I cross the border, my palms sweat and my heartbeat increases as I await the "Have you anything to declare?" question. We were ushered through without any hitch at all.

As we headed along Route 401 to London, I remembered Brent. I made a couple more idle threats about gas stations but never followed through. When we turned off the highway and headed for Guelph, we were only 10 miles from home. I got myself heated up one more time and told him that he and I would spend some time together as soon as we got home.

When we turned onto our street, our house was only six driveways up on the left side. With two driveways to go, Brent's voice came from the rear seat, as buttery as he could muster, "Gee, Dad, thanks for a great vacation." And then he added the coup de grace, "You're a great dad!" Now how could I spank a boy like that? You notice he didn't waste his praise back at Benton Harbor, at the border, or at London. No, he waited until I was the most vulnerable to it. He knew I would be relaxed and delighted to be home. He also was aware that if he blew it too soon, I was fully capable of getting myself all worked up again. By the way, Brent never did get spanked.

If you are unduly dependent on praise or approval, you can be sure that other people know this. There will be some who use it and others who abuse it. This dependence is a sign of weakness, but it is natural, and you should face it for what it is. You will have a daily battle and will never be free from it. The best you can do is recognize your own vulnerability, and then replace your weakness with His strength, to the glory and honor of God.

9

In
Search of
Blind Spots—III

"Thou wilt make known to me the path of life; in Thy presence is fullness of joy; in Thy right hand there are pleasures forever" (Psalm 16:11).

Last year we received very sad news. Our hearts ached as we were told how our friend of over 20 years had been shot to death, as he was holding a Bible study in a little village in northern Thailand.

Koos Fietje, only 38 years old, a husband and the father of three little children, gave his life in the service of his Lord. As a missionary with Overseas Missionary Fellowship (OMF), he had just returned to Thailand for his third term.

During his last visit with us in Florida, he shared with me his apprehension about returning. He could not explain it, but he had a sense of destiny that this term would be his last.

My mind kept wandering back to the times we spent working together in Kitchener, Ontario. I remembered the canoe trips, the laughter, and the fun. But I also remembered the day he shared with me God's call on his life. He was in awe that God could use him.

Koos has been graduated to glory. God showed him a path for his life and he is now in the presence of God where there are pleasures forevermore.

God has a plan for your life and a path He desires you to follow. It may not be the way that Koos had to trod, but whatever your path, there will be sacrifice involved. There is a world to be won.

But God can use us only as we desire to mature and to see ourselves more openly and honestly. We are encouraged to scrutinize ourselves. I hope these remaining introspective questions encourage you to self-examination.

Are You Really Interested in People?

"I thank my God in all my remembrance of you" (Philippians 1:3).

I hope there are people you care about so much that you can constantly thank God for them. If this is true, you will be eager to meet their needs and express a genuine interest in them.

My friend Don Richardson, author of *Peace Child*, tells a beautiful legend held by the Sawi people of New Guinea. They believed that at one time everyone lived under the crust of the earth. One day while hunting, a tribesman took careful aim and fired an arrow at a bird. Arrows are very precious to tribal people since it takes considerable time and effort to construct one. So he listened for the impact of the shot or for the sound of the arrow's fall. He heard neither and was confused. Groping in the darkness, he came to the huge tree where the bird had been. As he looked up, he saw a bright light. Curious, he climbed to the upper branches and looked out of a gaping hole which the arrow had made. What he saw was enough to completely overwhelm him— lush grasslands, mountains, rivers, sago palms, game, beautiful blue sky, clouds, and sunshine. All he could think of was to take his family with him to this paradise.

He climbed down the tree and hurried to the village to get his wife and children. They carried all they could to the tree. Just as they had made their way through the hole in the crust, he said, "It's not fair. I should go back and tell all my friends." He did and his friends brought their families. As everyone had made their way to the new paradise, the Sawi hunter was overcome with guilt and said, "It's still not fair. I should go back and tell everyone about our new home."

What a magnificent illustration of really caring about people! This concern does not stop with family, though it begins there, but is carried to friends, to strangers, and even to those who are difficult to love.

One who is truly interested in others will not see people as stepping stones, but will in honor prefer them. "Do not merely look out for your own personal interests, but also for the interests of others" (Philippians 2:4).

Do You Possess a Strong and Steady Will?

"Shadrach, Meshach, and Abed-nego answered and said to the king, 'O Nebuchadnezzar, we do not need to give you an answer concerning this. If it be so, our God whom we serve is able to deliver us from the furnace of blazing fire; and He will deliver us out of your hand, O king.

"'But even if He does not, let it be known to you, O king, that we are not going to serve your gods or worship the golden image that you have set up!'" (Daniel 3:16-18).

Do you finish the course you have set for yourself? Do you complete the tasks you start? Do you stick it out even in the hard times?

A few years ago our family was watching a world-class slalom skiing competition on TV. Among these very best skiers in the world was a young man from Taiwan, who taught us all a great lesson. He had no sooner started the course than he fell. This was to be the pattern of his entire descent. He would fall, then pick himself up and start again. The announcer told us this was the very first entry Taiwan ever had in World Cup skiing. It was a personal thrill to see the tenacity of this young man in finishing the course, since the odds cried out for him to quit.

The three Hebrew men who faced Nebuchadnezzar's fiery furnace had their minds made up. They held fast to a strong and steady will. Even as the king delivered his scoffing, "Who is the God who can deliver you out of my hands?" the three men stood firm. They told Nebuchadnezzar without hesitation that they were totally unafraid. If God wanted to deliver them, He could. "But if not, you may as well know we aren't going to worship your golden image anyway."

Such steadfast courage came from knowing God and knowing their full potential as children of the King. Can you sing, "Through it all I have learned to trust in Jesus"? Not until you are able to steadfastly state, "But if not" in an adverse circumstance do you have a clear picture of who you are in Him.

Do You Readily Forgive?

"And when you stand praying, forgive, if you have ought against any; that your Father also which is in heaven may forgive you your trespasses. But if you do not forgive, neither will your Father which is in heaven forgive your trespasses" (Mark 11:25-26, KJV).

The key word in this question is *readily* which the dictionary defines as "promptly, willingly, easily."

Almost every day someone does something which has the potential of hurting you or causing you to be offended. How do you handle it? What is it that demands you nurse your resentments? Pride, rotten old pride.

There is an axiom in our culture which says, "Don't get mad, get even." God says, "Forgive" and man says, "Get even." Who is correct? Obviously, God. But how do you accomplish this attitude in your life? Only through Christ!

I have known a few people who suffer from a martyr complex. These are folks who rather enjoy being hurt and offended by others. They enjoy complaining and engaging in self-pity. For being hurt legitimizes their negative outlook on life and gives credibility to the bitterness in their hearts. Whatever happened to forgiveness? What has happened that our hearts have become so hardened? That we feel we must exercise our rights?

Forgiveness does not depend on someone having to say he is sorry. If you rest your case on the fact that you are the injured party and someone else has to speak to you first, you are not practicing the love which comes from holy living.

There are no conditions to real love. Likewise there are no conditions to true forgiveness. A committed Christian does not have the liberty to say, "I will forgive you if...." Forgiveness is a precondition to answered prayer. If you are ever perplexed over why your prayers are not being answered, one possibility is that you lack a forgiving spirit.

"All things for which you pray and ask, believe that you have received them, and they shall be granted you" (Mark 11:24). It is exciting to think that whatever you pray for is yours if you only believe. But wait—don't get too excited. Here is the rest of the Scripture which gives the condition to the promise. "And whenever you stand praying, you *must* forgive anything that you are holding against anyone else" (Mark 11:25, PH). If you want God to really bless your life, so that you become the person He intends you to be, you must learn to readily forgive injuries done to you.

Are You an Optimistic High Achiever?
"Trust in the Lord, and do good; so shalt thou dwell in the land, and verily thou shalt be fed. Delight thyself also in the Lord; and He shall give thee the desires of thine heart. Commit thy way unto the Lord; trust also in Him; and He shall bring it to pass" (Psalm 37:3-5, KJV).

We must differentiate between reasonable and unreasonable optimism. The latter is as much of a problem as pessimism. Invariably, the fanatical optimist is a high-risk taker who has a total disregard for reality. Consequently, he always ends up as a low achiever. The following are the characteristics of high achievers:

● Moderate risk-taker. The high achiever is one who sets an achievable goal, not too high and not too low. The low achiever sets goals which are either too low or too high. From this vantage point he can respond by constantly achieving low goals—which generates poor performance, or by falling short of his unrealistically high goals—which generates zero performance. But the moderate risk-taker develops a sense of accomplishment and thrill which motivates him to further accomplishment.

● Immediate feedback. A high achiever needs immediate feedback of success or failure in order to evaluate his performance. He has learned that each situation should be analyzed in order to uncover ways of improving it. Once the high achiever has researched his performance, he is anxious to put the new conclusions into effect.

● Accomplishment. Perhaps it goes without saying that the high achiever must continue to accomplish. He has developed a pattern of success and keeps a steady eye on the goal—nothing wavering.

Not long ago we faced a minor, turned major, emergency at our church. We had scheduled a banquet for our returning summer missionaries and the entire church family, and then found out that our air conditioning unit would be overtaxed. With less than two weeks to go, two prominent businessmen in our fellowship took it on themselves to work night and day to do the impossible.

I shall not forget the comment one of them made as I anticipated the likelihood of not completing the task. I had suggested that they take it easy and go home. He looked at me and said, "Cliff, I don't know about you, but I am prepared to stay up from now until the banquet to get the job done. We haven't worked this hard just to come close." The high achiever persists to reach the possible dream.

● Preoccupation with the task. The high achiever becomes consumed with getting the job done. He has diligently followed through and does not rest easily until the task is completed to the best of his ability. Sometimes the high achiever may be viewed as somewhat distant or as a loner. But understanding how completely he gives himself to the task will help others to recognize this as a positive quality.

The Lord has promised to look after our needs. He also will bring to pass the desires of our heart. Can you be optimistic about that? But don't forget that your part includes trusting, doing, committing, and delighting. If you neglect any of these, you are exhibiting unreasonable optimism.

Do You Encourage People?
"Love never fails" (1 Corinthians 13:8).

So many times we miss out on opportunities to encourage people. Have you ever noticed how lightened your load is when someone takes the time to tell you that you are appreciated?

The Apostle Paul made this such a habit in his ministry that he truly was an encouragement to all. Whether he was behind prison walls or escaping a mob, he knew that love never fails. He knew that the trials and raging storms of life offer opportunities to manifest real love.

It is important for parents to take every opportunity to encourage their children. I had to go all the way to the jungles of Bolivia to be given a powerful illustration of how to encourage our young people and help them build strong and healthy self-images.

Missionary Gary Locy was assisting us on one of our summer mission projects. One weekend as we were on a hunting trip deep in the jungle, Gary and I sat and talked beside the glowing embers of a dying fire. He was sharing with me his heartache over the death of their oldest daughter. He told me story after story of how encouraging she had been and what a testimony her life was. This had affected the whole family and memories of her were a blessing to them now.

Throughout the evening Gary wove into the conversation many personal insights into his family life. One of them included an idea on how to build self-confidence in children. Often, he would wait till his children were sufficiently distant, but still within earshot, to tell his wife or a friend how proud he was of them. He would say it in a manner pretending to camouflage it, which merely exaggerated its importance. He would speak of their positive qualities and emphasize his love for them.

You can imagine how much his children love him. He had learned the secret that love never fails.

Do You Seek Out a Problem Person?

"Even if a man should be detected in some sin, my brothers, the spiritual ones among you should quietly get him back on the right path, not with any feeling of superiority but being yourselves on guard against temptation. Carry one another's burdens and so live out the Law of Christ" (Galatians 6:1-3, PH).

Do you know any problem people? They may have social problems, behavior problems, spiritual problems, or physical problems. The toughest for us are those which make us feel tense or embarrassed when we think about dealing with them.

We tend either to do nothing or to talk in circles, hoping that the individual will somehow catch on. There is a large body of counseling which falls under the umbrella of nondirective therapy. In other words, the therapist is there merely as a catalyst, to activate the individual's own perceptual and reasoning powers to discover both the problem and its attending solution.

This method is unreasonable at best, and impossible at worst. How unfair it is to allow one to struggle through life oblivious to the albatross around his neck. This is why we are commanded in Scripture to be faithful one to another and bear one another's burdens.

Carl Rogers, the grand patriarch of nondirective therapy, believes that if we simply have someone to share our problems with and if they are good listeners, our problems will somehow be resolved.

For many, philosphy of self-help has replaced the ministry of helping one another through the power of the Holy Spirit. What does Scripture say about this?

Do not merely look out for your own personal interests,
but also for the interests of others (Philippians 2:4).
Do not be haughty in mind, but associate with the lowly
(Romans 12:16).
Be devoted to one another in brotherly love; give
preference to one another in honor (Romans 12:10).
And concerning you, my brethren, I myself also am
convinced that you yourselves are full of goodness,
filled with all knowledge, and able also to admonish one
another (Romans 15:14).

Our counseling should be direct, honest, and
straightforward, believing God to do the work in a person's
life. We need to be faithful and encouraging. Such counseling may cause pain, but the pain from the surgeon's scalpel
always precedes the cure. Remember, no gain without pain.

Do You Compete or Complete?

"We have not ceased to pray for you . . . that you may walk in
a manner worthy of the Lord, to please Him in all respects,
bearing fruit in every good work and increasing in the knowledge of God" (Colossians 1:9-10).

I have always been a fierce competitor in athletics, and our
children have adopted this characteristic. When they were
little, I would play basketball with them in the driveway. Even
now I can clearly recall my feelings about my competitive
urge. I was caught on the horns of a dilemma—my nature
wanted to win; my fatherly concern wanted them to win.

This may not sound like much of a struggle, but it was for
me. Finally, Donna took me aside and encouraged me to let
them win more often to experience the excitement of victory.

Defeats, repeated day after day, occasion after occasion,
can shape a child's attitude. Any parent or significant adult
who is insensitive to a child's development may wonder in
later years why there is such an emotional distance between
them.

Our purpose is to complete, not to compete. This competition occurs not only between fathers and sons. I have listened to young girls share their concern over their mothers' competitive attitudes.

The Apostle Paul was driven by the desire to have everyone so increase in the knowledge of God that they would be presented as perfect, or mature, in Christ Jesus. Parents, teachers, significant adults, brothers, sisters, friends should be anxious to give, and to share, and to build up others.

Have you ever wondered why the world has never been evangelized? It is not because of a problem with our communication networks or language proficiency. Within 45 minutes after President Reagan was shot, the news had been carried all over the world. Why then has it taken 2,000 years to only partially communicate the good news of the Gospel?

One answer lies in the competitive, jealous nature of man. It is a sad but true commentary that the world has not been evangelized because we are too concerned about who gets the credit. We are so protective of our territory, our people, our tribes, our location, our little corner of the world, that we have lost the true vision and the passion of the great commission to go into all the world and make disciples.

In basketball terminology, if we are to evangelize the world in our generation, we must put on a "full-court press." Everyone has to do his very best, not being jealously concerned about what others are doing but concentrating intensely on his own responsibilities.

Do You Worship as You Work?

Serve the Lord with gladness;
come before His presence with singing.
Know ye that the Lord He is God;
it is He that hath made us, and not we ourselves;
we are His people and the sheep of His pasture.
Enter into His gates with thanksgiving,
and into His courts with praise (Psalm 100:2-4, KJV).

For many years this psalm seemed to be a beautiful rendition of how we should worship God with singing and praising. But then I asked myself why the sheep were gathered together within the gates and in the court. Was it merely to bleat sweet songs and to enjoy each other's fellowship? No!

The custom and culture of the day was to allow only the very best, the fattest, to enter into the courtyard as they were destined for the altar of sacrifice. As Christians, we have bargained for a cross. Let us therefore enter into His gates with thanksgiving and into his courts with praise, remembering that this is the age for crosses, not for crowns!

The story is told of an old missionary who was returning home to the United States after 50 years of service in India. He had buried his wife and two of their children there. He had lost contact with his relatives over the decades. Now his effectiveness was over and he left India. On the same ship was the adventurer, Teddy "Roughrider" Roosevelt, who had a large entourage with him. When the ship sailed into the New York harbor, crowds were waiting to greet Roosevelt— newspaper reporters were there, photographers, cheering crowds whistling and shouting.

The old missionary was the last passenger to leave. No one was there for him. He carried his one bag to a nearby hotel and checked in. His room had a single, shadeless light bulb dangling from the ceiling, a cot, no carpet, a broken mirror, and one wooden chair. He was depressed and discouraged. In his anguish he flung himself across the cot and with tears rolling down his cheeks, he cried out, "O God, I am so weary. God, when Mr. Roosevelt came home, there was such a crowd to meet him. Yet when I came home, there was no one. Why, God?"

Then just as surely as Paul heard the Lord on the Damascus Road, this old missionary warrior heard the still small voice assuring him, "You're not home yet, Son—you're not home yet."

Conclusion
"Indeed, it is useless to spread the net in the eyes of any bird" (Proverbs 1:17).

One of our favorite programs on TV was "The Wild Kingdom" with Marlin Perkins. On one particular program they were attempting to capture an eagle by luring him with a decoy rabbit. The idea was to roll out a large net and keep dragging the rabbit back and forth across it. They did this for a whole day until they realized that the eagle had not only seen them but had seen the net too.

We will not fall victim and be lured into danger if we are able to see the traps that are laid before us. The purpose of these introspective questions has been to show us our dangerous blind spots. Each of the questions demands self-examination. By no means are any of the subjects exhausted. Nor is that necessary. The eagle didn't have to know every detail about the net and its would-be captors. It did have to know enough to sense the danger.

"Thy Word have I treasured in my heart, that I may not sin against Thee" (Psalm 119:11).

10

Can Self-Image Be Changed?

"By this all men will know that you are My disciples, if you have love for one another" (John 13:35).

Our home in central Florida is less than one hour from many major tourist attractions. When we have a free day, it is sometimes hard to choose between Disney World, Sea World, Circus World, and the others. However, my personal favorite is Sea World, since I am fascinated by the curious exhibits of sea life.

If you have been to Sea World, you remember Shamu, the killer whale. What a show he puts on! It is nearly unbelievable the way this magnificent creature launches out of the water, twists in midair, does a back flip and comes crashing down backward on the surface of the pool in exactly the right spot to spray half the spectators.

I have never seen a killer whale free in its natural environment, my only experience with them being at Sea World. However, I am reasonably confident that whales don't spend their time doing back flips and somersaults. I have sometimes wished we could ask Shamu, "How did you do that flip? Did you ever dream about being able to do those tricks?" If Shamu could answer me, I'm sure he would say that he never would have thought it possible for a killer whale to do tricks since he never saw one doing them.

Assuming we are correct in Shamu's answer, we are faced with the question: Do killer whales have the capacity to do things they never thought possible? Yes. Well then, what causes them to be able to do things that are not natural to them? What catalyst has surfaced these latent talents?

The answer lies not with Shamu but with someone Shamu now trusts, his trainer. Even though Shamu didn't know he could do tricks, his trainer knew he could.

Shamu did not lack the capability to do any of these things. What Shamu lacked was a person to reveal his possibilities and then instill confidence in him so that he could realize them. This is exactly what the trainer did. During long and tedious hours, he developed a positive relationship with Shamu. He was keenly observant of Shamu's progress and reinforced and encouraged him every step of the way. Although Shamu was totally unaware of the goal, he was willing to perform behaviors foreign to his natural inclinations so long as he received reinforcement or encouragement. This did not mean that Shamu was never disciplined. What it does mean, however, is that discipline was not the dominant system used to effect behavioral change. Discipline is always more acceptable and successful if it is not isolated from encouragement and love. Through the various techniques the trainer used, he changed Shamu's self-image. And this happened primarily through love and encouragement.

Love Never Fails

At every seminar I hold, I am asked one question, though it comes in many forms: "Can I do anything for my husband or my wife who has a low self-image?" Yes, a thousand times yes, but it will require devoted love. It will demand patience that only those who really love can endure.

Some time ago I was conducting two evening seminars at Naperville North High School in Illinois. In the audience was a family, a husband, wife, and son, who had recently suffered the loss of their older son to cancer. Doug and Joan White told me how for the last several years of Curt's life they shared the duty of alternately spending the night with him in Children's Hospital in Chicago. They were willing to sacrifice time with each other for the love that Curt needed.

I remembered meeting the White family about a year before at the national Christian high school basketball championships in Wisconsin. They were there to spend time with their close friends, the Cramers, who are members of our church in Longwood, Florida. I shall never forget the servant love of Doug as he carried Curt or made sure that while he was in his wheelchair he could see the game. The night of the seminar Doug expressed his love for Curt when he said, "Cliff, it was no problem. We would do it all again. It was our life and he was our son and we miss him dearly, even though we are delighted to know that Curt is in heaven with his Lord." Doug then prayed, thanking God for Curt's life and death, and asking that the family now would bring glory to God and be faithful witnesses for the Lord Jesus Christ.

There is only one thing that Scripture says never fails—absolutely never. Love never fails. I have been accused of taking this principle to the extreme, but I still conclude that love is God's way to solve any problem. It was the way He chose to redeem mankind. If we use God's method of loving people, they will change. All of God's creation responds to love, encouragement, and tender loving care.

Christianity in Action

There is a great deal of skepticism among non-Christians about Christianity and, frankly, I can't blame them. It is largely due to the fact that while they have observed many counterfeits, they have never seen real Christianity in action. The one authenticating mark of a true believer is that he possesses the fruit of the Spirit—love, joy, peace, long-suffering, gentleness, goodness, faith, meekness, and self-control.

Even if we were to put a colon after the word *love,* we would still have a complete definition of the fruit of the Spirit, for love is lived out in the other qualities.

When we first moved to Florida, it was midsummer. We saw fruit trees in our yard, but since I am not much of a horticulturist, we had to wait until late October for the fruit, before we could conclusively say what kinds of trees they were.

This is exactly what Jesus taught His disciples, "By this all men will know that you are My disciples, if you have love for one another" (John 13:35). God's love instills confidence into His children. We do not have to be afraid. "If God be for us, who can be against us?" (Romans 8:31, KJV)

We come to grips with the fact that we are not perfect, just forgiven, and that we are not judged according to man's standard of success but according to God's measuring stick of faithfulness. We will be judged to the measure that we are faithful with the gifts and talents God has blessed us with. Much shall be required of those to whom God has given much.

Satan remains determined to block every opportunity of growth in the lives of God's children. If Satan can stunt our growth, he gains at least a partial victory. Anyone imprisoned in a low self-image has fallen victim to the wiles of the enemy. We are our brothers' keepers and we must harness ourselves to the responsibility of becoming part of solutions to problems. In response to the discussion about who would be the greatest among the disciples, Jesus answered, "Whoever wishes to become great among you shall be your servant" (Mark 10:43). It is the servant heart that draws response. The anthenticating mark of the servant is love. His equipment—a servant's towel.

Under the rule of Diocletian in the fourth century, an order was issued for all Christians to be put to death. Phocas, of Sinope, was high on the list issued by the magistrates. When the officers arrived in Sinope they were exhausted, hungry, and thirsty after their long journey. Phocas, whose home was just inside the city, made it his custom to welcome all strangers and put them up for the night. He did this so that he could introduce them to his Lord and Saviour. He was anxious to meet their spiritual needs by first earning their trust and confidence through sharing his home with them.

He noticed that these officers needed encouragement. In the course of their conversation, Phocas asked them what brought them to Sinope. It was then he learned that they had orders from Rome to execute a local Christian named Phocas. Undaunted by the news, he continued to show them love and hospitality. That evening by the heat of the fire, Phocas shared with them the claims of the Lord Jesus Christ. The officers, not realizing who he was, were impressed and thanked their host as they retired for the night.

Phocas did not go to bed but prayed fervently all night— not that his life be spared but that he remain a faithful witness to glorify God. When morning came, Phocas had a meal ready for the men. After breakfast he took the officers outside where they saw a grave which Phocas had dug during the night. They did not understand until Phocas told them who he was. They were shocked, and wondered why he had not escaped to spare his life. When the officers were unwilling to fulfill their orders, Phocas reminded them that Diocletian would execute them for permitting his escape. He wanted them to realize that death was not his foe nor the grave his enemy. He willingly gave his life and his only desire was for his captors to meet his Saviour. They had seen real Christianity in action.

Essential Characteristics of True Love

Let us take a journey to the land of true love to examine the spiritual heritage of a child of the King. If you will manifest these in your life you will have found the secret of real power.

"Love is patient, love is kind, and is not jealous; love does not brag and is not arrogant, does not act unbecomingly; it does not seek its own, is not provoked, does not take into account a wrong suffered, does not rejoice in unrighteous-ness, but rejoices with the truth; bears all things, believes all things, hopes all things, endures all things. Love never fails" (1 Corinthians 13:4-8a).

• Love is patient. How much easier it is to punish than to correct. It takes less time and demands less emotional ener-gy. How much easier when people have offended us to give them a piece of our mind or silently ignore them than to talk with them in love. How much easier it is to retaliate than to suffer the wrong done to us. Retaliation is pride—we just don't want anyone to get the best of us.

Little children respond to the love of a parent who knows how to encourage as well as to discipline. Both are love if our hearts are pure. Husbands and wives desperately need patient and long-suffering love. A husband who lacks the drive to initiate or to attempt new things needs the patient love of a submissive, tender wife. If the wife continues to pressure her husband by constantly initiating and planning everything, his natural tendency will be to fall into the shad-ows. The wife who desires her husband to take the lead may feel frustrated. But from his perspective, as long as there is one driver at the wheel, he will see no need for a second. The wife must be willing to sacrifice and subordinate her drive until the husband gains his emotional footing. Only through her patient love and encouragement will he change.

Likewise, the wife needs the assuring strength that only her husband can provide. He needs to compliment her be-fore their children and friends. He needs to encourage her to develop her strengths. He needs to patiently provide her op-portunities for growth and for new experiences. He should never compare her with other women, but should tenderly protect her from those things which could hurt her emotion-ally. Patience is the willingness to wait for God's perfect tim-ing and to be ready to encourage at all times.

• Love is kind. Love is not love merely because it is pa-tient. It is love because in its patience it is kind. I personally know people who could be classified as long-suffering and yet exhibit bitterness and hostility. They seethe inside, but endure by sheer determination and obstinacy. To endure with the love of Christ means a tenderness of attitude and behavior that does not feel resentment.

I have a dear friend who recently suffered a tremendous business collapse which was directly related to another individual. My friend had gone into partnership with a well-known person who is a Christian. Unfortunately, this individual took advantage at a very vulnerable time and left my friend virtually destitute. It seemed impossible that such a thing could occur but it did. My friend could have defended his position legally but he chose not to do so. He did not feel he had the right to expose the other individual, since doing so would have clearly damaged the testimony of the Lord. He did, however, share his feelings privately. Even a year later he was unwilling to do anything that could negatively affect the person and the organization. Was he foolish? Or was he showing the love of kindness and suffering long for Christ's sake?

Do other people's failures annoy you or challenge you? Are you challenged to pray and build them up in the faith, or do you take delight in exposing their sins? God is not initially interested in exposure as much as He is in cleansing and repentance. Let us accept the challenge of failure as an opportunity to love and be kind rather than expose.

● Love is not jealous. What a contrast there was in the last days of Jesus' ministry on earth—He had set His face toward Jerusalem and His disciples were squabbling over positions in the kingdom. He was facing the cross and they were envisaging crowns and thrones. He was marching headlong into self-sacrifice and death and they were bargaining over prominence.

The love of Christ is the only love that can produce a life without rivalry and jealousy. This love actually rejoices over the blessings of others. Paul wrote to Christians in Rome, "Rejoice with those who rejoice, and weep with those who weep" (12:15). Weeping with others is easy, but rejoicing with others is very difficult, particularly when they are rejoicing over the thing you wanted the most.

Something most wonderful that God has accomplished in our home is a genuine rejoicing for each other. There is real excitement when one has done well, even if another has not received the same glory. And our children have learned to weep for each other and to hurt when one hurts. Not everything in life is equitable. Some of our children have received more attention and opportunity than others.

I know of homes where the children literally despise the successes of their brothers and sisters. They have no time for each other. Why? It is hard to write a definitive answer, but the initial problem must fall at the parents' feet.

Sometimes husbands and wives are envious of each other. I have counseled with wives who are so jealous of their husbands' successes that they relish in their failures. Likewise, I have met with husbands who are furious with their wives' abilities to organize and get things done. I even know parents who have a hard time dealing with their children's accomplishments. You can be sure of this one thing—if you are envious, you will never see a positive change in the one who needs your help. The Bible tells us to esteem others more highly than ourselves. This is the mark of the servant's heart.

● Love does not brag and is not arrogant. The Lord Jesus said, "Whosoever exalts himself shall be humbled; and whoever humbles himself shall be exalted" (Matthew 23:12).

The love of Christ does not lead a Christian to be a braggart or a blowhard. But yet some are. Why? The flesh demands attention. Pride in the heart cannot naturally do any other than seek the aggrandizement of self.

There are some people of whom it can be rightly said, "If you want to find out how good he is just ask him." Love brags on other people. Donna and I were in a home not long ago where our host said, "I just love to brag on my wife— she's wonderful!" How do you think his wife felt? Do you think she is secure in their relationship? Do you think she feels confident in herself to try new things? Absolutely.

If you want to see others change, brag on them. Tell others about their accomplishments. Be proud of them and let them know it. Encourage them to get involved in growth activities at school or church and be sure to support them, no matter what happens. Bragging on yourself destroys relationships. Bragging on others strengthens relationships as well as encouraging a healthy and strong self-image.

• Love does not act unbecomingly. The Apostle Paul was concerned about how Christians would be perceived by others. Some Christians think it makes no difference whether they speak bluntly or tactlessly, so long as they speak the truth. There certainly does need to be etiquette in the Christian life. It is most unbecoming when honesty preys on love and when candor is more important than sympathy. If these patterns are characteristic of your life, you can be sure there is a lack of balance in your spiritual life. Love is not without discrimination. Love is not tactless. Love is not cruelly blunt. Love behaves itself in a manner befitting the occasion.

I know a man who constantly criticizes his wife in public for everything. He does so in a loud "joking" manner. People have laughed at his sick humor for years at the expense of his introverted wife. Such behavior is unbecoming. It is not love. It will certainly destroy potential development. Love is consistent in behavior and always seeks to cover the rough spots in another's life rather than to laugh and deride.

• Love does not seek its own. Selfishness lies at the heart of all evil in the world, whether it is within nations or families or denominations or mission boards or churches or individuals. Unselfishness is the hallmark of love.

Today more than ever we are hearing about rights: civil rights, human rights, equal rights, rights, rights, rights! So much so that rights have become rites. We read everywhere about civil rights being violated. What has happened to a justice system that allows mobsters, rapists, murderers, child molesters, and other violent offenders to be free, merely because their rights were violated according to the law?

What about the victims' rights?

A society can be torn apart by enough people demanding to have their own way. Here is a question by which you can judge your quality of love. Can you accept opposition to your viewpoint or decision without considering it a personal affront and reacting accordingly?

Selfishness will destroy the love between a husband and wife. It will nullify the bond between parent and child. It will hinder the development of friendships and will destroy the integrity of your testimony for the Lord.

Unselfishness is the love that only Christ could give. It will change lives—including yours.

● Love is not provoked. Self-seeking individuals tend to be easily provoked when their self-love is not satisfied. Love is not easily irritated. My dad used to say that we could measure our emotional strength by the things which irritate us. What bothers you? Really gets you upset?

If someone is rubbing your fur the wrong way, then turn around. I have learned that if I get rubbed the wrong way, it is my fault. Why? Because I shouldn't have a wrong way to be rubbed.

Next time you are driving your car, see how easily you get provoked. Maybe all it takes is for some little, old lady to be struggling along at 30 MPH in a 45 MPH zone. Or perhaps it is someone who fails to signal and you have to slow down. Or maybe it is a broken traffic light or a driver who refuses to let you pass.

Are you provoked at your child's performance in school? Are you provoked because he has no interest in music or sports? Are you provoked because your husband did not get the promotion? Are you provoked because God has not chosen to lift your burden or lighten your load? Are you provoked because you are easily provoked?

Love does not need to display irritation. Love recognizes imperfection even in oneself and therefore more readily tolerates it in others. Love does not allow a selfish display of bad temper because this would have damaging effects on others. Love develops a very high threshold for irritation. Only if we are armed with this kind of love can we possibly help effect a positive change in another's life.

• Love does not take into account a wrong suffered. Love certainly does not nurture the memories of wrongs done to us. Love is not predisposed to think the worst of anyone. Love has learned never to prejudge or take the word of a third party. Love not only controls the tongue but also controls what we choose to remember. All this is an obvious act of the will.

As spouses, parents, and friends, we need to be willing to forgive wrongs we have suffered. If we are able to do so, we will be awesome examples of love that thinks no evil. This will speak volumes to those around us. Children ought to see living proof that the love of Christ is real in their parents' lives, that husbands and wives can forgive each other unconditionally.

• Love does not rejoice in unrighteousness. When you learn that someone in a prominent position has been found guilty of wrongdoing, what is your reaction? Love is never glad when wrong is done. Have you ever been guilty of saying, "It serves him right—he deserved that"? Have you ever thought about what we deserve? Love does not think it "cute" when a child disobeys. Love is not blind. Love is faithful in the lives of our loved ones. A parent who truly loves a child corrects him rather than allowing him to grow up as a selfish, obnoxious adult.

• Love bears all things. There are two meanings for *bear*, both of which are implicit in this context. First, it means to support in the sense of holding something or someone else up. Love elevates others and is a support system when needed. Second, love throws a cloak of silence over difficult situations. Love provides a roof of security. Love puts up a shelter to shield, cover, and protect others. The best way to put out a fire is to cover it.

Bearing all things includes the successes and joys of others as well as their faults. Love knows how to praise others for their good qualities. The cloak of silence here is speaking specifically about the tongue. Do you find yourself anxious to spread the latest gossip? Or to hear the latest gossip?

● Love believes all things. Does this mean that we are to believe everything that others tell us? By no means! But we should be predisposed to believe. Here is a good rule of thumb: Love inspired by God always serves the good of the other person. There is no benefit to anyone if you allow a person to believe he has gotten away with lies or dishonesty. You do not help a disobedient child by pretending to believe his lies or by not taking time to discipline him for the lies. Love believes all things that are true.

If children raised in a Christian home are still rebellious when they become adults, there was a problem in the home and it started with the parents. Proverbs 22:6 says, "Train up a child in the way that he should go, even when he is old he will not depart from it." This promise was not given to ease the pain in the heart of a parent. It is merely a statement of fact to be examined carefully. The Scripture is saying that whatever way you train a child, when he is an adult he will not depart from it. Again this is more evidence for the importance of love in building a strong and healthy biblically based self-image of a child.

● Love hopes all things. Hope is one of the outstanding characteristics of the Gospel. Our blessed hope is the joy we have in knowing that Jesus is coming again. Our hope rests secure because we know how it all will end. This is the vision of hope we need to instill into our children, spouses, and friends. Encouragement can turn despair into joy, confusion into tranquillity, loneliness into fullness of life, and fear into faith. To see hope and possibility can help people change the course of their lives. Are you reasonably optimistic? Do you see light at the end of the tunnel and know it is not a train? Instill hope into your family and they will respond with enthusiasm. Hope will give anyone a new identity, a new self-image.

● Love endures all things. The word *endure* means to

hold on under a burden. Grip tightly, sink your teeth in, and give it all you've got. This is the final ingredient before the conclusion, "Love never fails." When love has tried everything, and has exercised all of its resources and still has not achieved its aim, even then love will endure. It will suffer patiently and optimistically.

When all else fails, keep on loving. God has told us that love never fails. I would rather put my trust in His promises than in man's logic. If you continue to exercise the agape love of Christ, even though the way seems impossible, He will guarantee the happiness and contentment in your life and in the lives of those you love.

The only way to change your self-image is by love. If you are imprisoned in a negative self-image, try agape love. Follow our Lord's example and begin to give yourself to others. Help others to fulfill their hopes and realize their potential, and you will also change. Your change will be directly proportional to your faithful employment of the love of Christ.

11

Where Are You Heading?

*"The time of my departure has come. I have fought
the good fight, I have finished the course, I have kept
the faith; in the future there is laid up for me the
crown of righteousness, which the Lord, the righteous Judge, will award to me on that day; and not
only to me, but also to all who have loved His appearing" (2 Timothy 4:6-8).*

I am always amazed and perplexed at how easily we can
become diverted from our goals. I am not sure it is laziness,
for I have seen too many people spending many long hours
going absolutely nowhere.

One morning while sitting outside under the beautiful
Florida sky and sunshine, I noticed a little insect and
watched it, totally fascinated by its movement. It was in such
a hurry, scurrying about, running in circles, traveling for the
entire 15 minutes within one square foot of ground. It
climbed up and down the same twigs dozens of times but
never got very far. Just as it seemed to really be moving
along, it got sidetracked and turned suddenly back to where
it had been. But when it returned, it continued its frenzied
pace, yet never really went anywhere.

This reminds me of people who wander aimlessly through life, never resting, never evaluating where they are going, but relentlessly running in circles. Part of the insect's pattern was the sudden redirection of its path. It seemed to be chasing every new possibility with a sense of desperation—a sort of last hope.

People need to focus on the goals which most suit their needs and then resist and reject the distractions which will inevitably come. Otherwise, like the insect they will spend their lives trapped in perpetual motion, going nowhere and accomplishing nothing.

Definition of Intelligence

In the early part of the 20th century, Alfred Binet was researching human intelligence and means of testing it. After years of research, he developed a definition of intelligence which was accepted by educators. Binet defined intelligence as the following three abilities working together:

- The ability to take and maintain a definite direction.
- The ability to make adaptations to achieve the goal.
- The ability to evaluate and correct oneself.

Clearly, this definition deals with goal-setting.

The first ability contains three key words—take, maintain, and definite. Most people begin goal-oriented projects, but few finish them. Why? There are two reasons. First, they never learn the discipline of maintaining, of keeping their eyes on the goal. Second, they don't have a definite, clear-cut goal in mind. The goal is fuzzy, never stated precisely. If either of these reasons is present, the chances of ever achieving the desired goal are very, very slim.

The Goal Setting Process

A goal is defined as a statement of direction, intent, or purpose. When a goal is a statement of direction, you have a clear idea where you are going and when and how you intend to get there. A goal also gives you a general idea about where you are not going. As you gather data and gain more experience, you make your selected direction increasingly specific. It is possible to think about goals within the following four dimensions:

● Explicit/Implicit. Explicit means clearly expressed, developed in detail, distinctly stated, definite. Implicit means not clearly stated or expressed but meant.

● Small/Large. This is a relative dimension based on the size of the goal.

● Reality Based/Fantasy Based. Reality goals are goals based on present capacity or expected future potential. Fantasy goals are those which, according to the reality of the present, would be classified as dreams and private desires. Fantasy goals are generally hidden, seldom shared.

● Short Term/Long Term. This is a relative dimension based on time. Long-term goals are beyond the immediate future, and should be influencing our present behavior. Short-term goals are calculated to assist us in accomplishing the long-term goals.

The first two dimensions describe what the goal is. Their purpose is to give a clear picture of exactly what it is you want to accomplish.

For example, if you say that the major goal of your life is to glorify God, then you are implicitly stating that your behavior should conform to that goal. Although you do not explicitly state in clear detail what your behavior will be, you imply a great deal that is generally understood. But here is the caution. Implicit goals can always generate confusion due to various interpretations.

The third dimension, Reality Based/Fantasy Based, describes how you will accomplish the goal.

Let us suppose that you are a housewife who has always dreamed about writing a book. But your present situation—caring for three small children and a busy husband, and your heavy church involvement—militates against your dream. This would be fantasy. Fantasy goals are not impossible in the long term; but according to present circumstances they are. When we fail to recognize the distinction between reality and fantasy goals, we can become frustrated and even irritated with our present situation.

This is exactly what Satan desires for us. When we are in torment and not content with the present, we are at war emotionally. Reality is the major determining factor in the entire goal-setting process. We should dream the impossible dream, but we should be willing to exhibit the patience its fulfillment demands. Exciting dreams will not be realized overnight. And it requires deep commitment to not get pushed off track.

The fourth dimension has to do with when the goal will be accomplished. Long-term goals are essentially related to fantasy goals in that they can not, for one reason or another, be accomplished immediately. But the successful attainment of the long-term goal is directly related to accomplishing many short-term goals.

For example, a young boy dreams of becoming a doctor. This fantasy goal can be realized only when it is examined as a long series of short-term goals. As a high school student, the boy must set reality goals such as earning high grades in science, graduating in the top 10 percent of the class. Then he must be accepted at a university that has a record of getting its students into med school. Once again grades are utmost. Each grade can be broken down to each examination, to each midterm, and even to each lecture. The student's goal should be to attend every lecture and listen intently to gain the most from it. In belaboring this point, we see that fantasy goals are realized only when we achieve the sometimes insignificant reality goals of everyday life.

Binet's second ability is making adaptations to achieve the goal. Notice it does not say to make adaptations in the goal, but rather to make adaptations in our behavior to achieve the goal.

A goal for every believer is to be involved in evangelizing the world. We can argue about it, debate it, or hold conferences to discuss it, but the fact still remains that we have been sent forth to the ends of the earth to make disciples.

The strategy is to win the world. But how? What tactics do we employ? Where will we employ them and where will they be most effective? Will certain tactics always be effective? Has the world changed sufficiently in the last 2,000 years to alter how we should go about making disciples?

Obviously, the key word in the second ability is *adaptation*. The adaptations are always in the tactics. We should not narrow our vision because we meet a roadblock, but decide how we can move around the roadblock or remove it. Our orders have not been changed. The Commander-in-Chief still says, "Go ye into all the world."

A few years ago, *Time* magazine ran an article about a Japanese soldier who was found roaming the jungles of a Philippine Island, 30 years after the end of World War II. On several occasions over the years, people had tried to convince him to give up and return home to Japan. Leaflets were even dropped from airplanes, but he remained adamant that he would not leave his post until his commander changed his orders.

The authorities located the aged officer who was responsible for the orders. Dressed in full World War II uniform, he came face to face with the loyal soldier. The old commander thanked the soldier for his faithfulness to duty. Then he changed his orders and they returned home together.

Our Commander-in-Chief, the Lord Jesus, has not changed our orders. The goal is still to evangelize the world to the remotest corners of the earth.

When we set personal goals, we should work hard to achieve them rather than change them. We should respond creatively to the roadblocks rather than passively accept them. Change the tactics, not the goal.

Binet's third ability is the capacity to evaluate and correct oneself. This is never easy. Perhaps in the purest sense of evaluation and correction, it is never possible. Yet searching for our blind spots is essential if we are to become great leaders. There is a direct relationshp between successful leadership and being able to evaluate and correct ourselves.

The Importance of Goal-Setting

● Personal commitment. We do not do the things we know. We only do the things we believe. We also only commit ourselves to those things we believe. We set a goal because we feel a conviction about something. However, we will not reach the goal until we commit ourselves to its attainment.

On May 25, 1961 John F. Kennedy told Congress, "This nation should commit itself to achieving the goal, before this decade is out, of landing a man on the moon and returning him safely to the earth."

Because of President Kennedy's deep sense of personal commitment, he assured the accomplishment of the goal. His encouragement and belief were the ingredients necessary to create a climate of success.

Acts 9 records the details of Paul's encounter with the Lord Jesus on the road to Damascus. In immediate response to a blinding light, Paul "trembling and astonished said, 'Lord, what wilt Thou have me to do?'" (v. 6, KJV) Throughout the remainder of his life, Paul's eyes were focused on the Light of heaven. He was committed, dedicated to a cause larger than himself. He was able, by the grace of God, to end his life with the full knowledge that he had kept the faith and that his reward, a crown of righteousness, awaited him in glory.

What a thrill it is to give yourself to a task and to work tirelessly to it's completion. That is a satisfied life.

● Internal motivation. One can only be motivated in the short term by extrinsic motivation. However, external motivation will not be sufficient to sustain the drive necessary to overcome obstacles and conflicting emotions in the long run. It has been said that there is no gain without pain. In any exercise program it is only when the sit-ups begin to hurt that anything of value is accomplished. It is not until you are willing to sacrifice recreation time for study time that academic achievement becomes a reality.

What was it that motivated Paul? What concepts had he

internalized to the point that nothing else mattered but the reaching of a lost world?

In his second letter to the Christians at Corinth, he gives a clear insight into his motives for serving the Lord Jesus so faithfully:

"Therefore also we have as our ambition, whether at home or absent, to be pleasing to Him. For we must all appear before the Judgment Seat of Christ, that each one may be recompensed for his deeds in his body, according to what he has done, whether good or bad.

"Therefore, knowing the fear of the Lord, we persuade men, but we are made manifest to God; and I hope that we are made manifest also in your consciences. We are not again commending ourselves to you, but are giving you an occasion to be proud of us, that you may have an answer for those who take pride in appearance, and not in heart. For if we are beside ourselves, it is for God; if we are of sound mind, it is for you.

"For the love of Christ controls us, having concluded this, that one died for all, therefore all died; and He died for all, that they who live should no longer live for themselves, but for Him who died and rose again on their behalf" (2 Corinthians 5:9-15).

In this text we find the five factors which motivated Paul to a life of service and endurance in the face of severe suffering.

In verse 9 we read, "to be pleasing to Him." Paul was anxious to hear the Lord say, "Well done, good and faithful slave.... Enter into the joy of your Master" (Matthew 25:21). He desired the approval of his Master. In other writings Paul expressed fear of becoming a "castaway." He was not fearful of losing his salvation, but he was terrified of becoming a has-been and being placed on the shelf, unfit for service. He was obsessed with pleasing the Saviour.

In verse 10 we find the second motive: "We must all appear before the Judgment Seat of Christ." Here Paul was referring to the Bema seat of Christ, the time of the evaluation. This judgment will not determine our eternal destiny, but will be an examination of our words and deeds. Every unconfessed sin will be exposed, as will all the works of the flesh. Paul was determined to have his work count for eternity.

In verse 11 we read, "Knowing the fear of the Lord, we persuade men." Paul was passionate for the lost. As a Jewish rabbi, he was well-grounded in the Old Testament Scriptures which portrayed vividly the terror of the Lord. Paul knew for sure that God would be faithful to His Word. He knew that outside of repentance, and a belief in the redemptive work of Jesus Christ, a soul would be eternally damned. He knew that salvation demanded a confession of sin and an acceptance of Jesus as Saviour. He was motivated by "the terror of the Lord."

Verse 14 shares the foundation for all that motivated him—"For the love of Christ controls us." Overwhelmed by the Lord Jesus, Paul shared with the Galatian churches these words: "I have been crucified with Christ, and it is no longer I who live, but Christ lives in me; and the life which I now live in the flesh I live by faith in the Son of God, who loved me, and delivered Himself up for me" (Galatians 2:20).

Paul was motivated by the fact that Jesus Christ, the Son of God, would give Himself for him. Paul was quick to add, "and not for me only but unto all them also that love His appearing."

Verse 15 declared why Paul was taking the Gospel to the ends of the earth: "He died for all." Paul knew the Gospel was for everyone, Jew and Greek, male and female, and that everyone should hear it. Oswald J. Smith, the great missionary statesman and founder of The People's Church in Toronto, was a modern-day Paul when he said, "Why should anyone hear the Gospel twice before everyone has heard it once?"

• Self-Discipline. Habit-formation requires strong self-discipline. Even bad habits demand the discipline to practice, drill, and rehearse. I am told that the first few cigarettes one smokes taste awful. But because smoking is a goal, the smoker endures the pain and disciplines himself to practice, drill, and rehearse. Before long he smokes with competence and confidence. Soon it is a habit.

Yes, even bad habits and sin require discipline. Similarly, we should strive and stretch ourselves beyond our grasp for those positive habits which include the discipline of setting and attaining goals of lasting value.

Three Successful Goal-Setting Principles

Goals should be attainable, measurable, and written.

● Attainable. One of the laws of learning is the principle of reinforcement. Behaviors which are reinforced or rewarded are most likely to recur. If we are not being rewarded for certain behaviors, then it is clear those behaviors will cease. Therefore, we should be careful that we set attainable goals. If we do not, we will become discouraged and the process of building success habits will cease.

Because a long-range goal is not readily attainable, a program of short-range and intermediate-range goals should be established. This will lead to the eventual attainment of the long-range goals.

Too many people have tried to achieve the "big" goal before they are ready, and as a consequence, have failed miserably. This has caused them to abandon their dreams and live futile lives. How unfortunate, when all that was needed was to take the steps necessary for success! It is just like climbing a ladder. You keep your eyes fixed at the top (the goal) while climbing one rung at a time.

● Measurable. If a person sets a goal to lose weight, will the goal be attained if he loses only one pound? Absolutely! Since the goal is merely to lose weight, any loss accomplishes it.

The more specific our goals, the more certain we are of their achievement. If the goal is to lose 25 pounds and the short-term goal is to lose a pound every two days, then the one-pound weight loss is a vital step toward the goal. The short-term goals keep people on track by creating a climate of reinforcement.

• Written. Whenever we record our goals in writing we are making a commitment to ourselves. We no longer can rationalize or procrastinate, for our goals are in front of us to remind us. And if we share our goals with a close friend, we are motivated even more. If the goal is attainable and measurable, the process of putting it in writing merely fortifies the reality of the accomplishment.

What are we to do when we do not achieve a goal? How can we be sure that a goal is really attainable?

It is hard for us as parents to see our children struggle with accomplishment. Our hearts ache and we want to jump in and help them. Unfortunately, we do so sometimes, at the expense of the personal growth of our children. By constantly finishing their projects for them, completing those tough math problems and doing their household chores, we are robbing them of opportunities to develop emotional toughness. If our children do not learn the principles of taking and maintaining a definite direction in the face of any circumstance, then we have failed them miserably. We have created emotional cripples who would rather quit than face any Goliath in their lives.

The story is told of a lady who had a greenhouse attached to her home. She loved to spend time in it and one day noticed a cocoon growing on a branch of a small tree. She continued to watch it daily for she was fascinated by the various stages of its development. She learned that it was the transformation of the magnificent Emperor moth.

Early one morning she saw the cocoon shaking and noticed that the moth was attempting to squeeze itself through a very tiny hole on the top. The moth made numerous attempts at escape but the hole seemed far too small. Finally the lady succumbed to her feelings of sympathy for the moth and decided to help. With a pin she made the hole larger and the next day the moth easily crawled out. The lady was eagerly anticipating the spreading of the wings of this beautiful Emperor moth. Instead she saw the moth fall from the top of the cocoon to the greenhouse floor, unable to reach its potential, unable to be what God had intended. Why? The tiny hole which was creating the crisis and conflict was necessary for the full development of the moth. It was the Creator's plan for the moth to have to squeeze through that unbearably tight spot in order that the wings and body would be stretched to the maximum. Only then would the moth be ready for its first solo flight. Only then would the wings be strong enough to bear the burden of the body of the moth.

The Creator's plan includes our having to pass through many pressure points and tight spots to become the individuals He has planned for us to be.

Where are you heading? Have you made clear and concrete goals for today, for the week, for the month, for this year, for your life? And how do you intend to get where you are going?

These goal-setting principles will help you only if you use them. The Word of God teaches that if we lack wisdom, we should ask for it and the Lord will give it to us (James 1:5). If we are confused about a decision, we should remember this principle: "Commit your works to the Lord, and your plans will be established" (Proverbs 16:3).

12

Design for Successful Living

"No good thing does He withhold from those who walk uprightly" (Psalm 84:11).

In this verse the promise is followed by a condition. This is an order that God never changes. He has promised not to withhold anything from us, if it is for our good, if we walk or live according to His precepts. If we are walking in the Spirit and manifesting the fruit of the Spirit, then we can rest assured that God will cause all the circumstances of our lives to be good for us.

One day while conducting a seminar in a large downtown Chicago hotel, I met a black insurance executive named Art Miller. After the seminar he wanted to speak to me and share from his childhood. He told me that one of his real heroes in life was his cousin who had fallen into so many problems that his life was a mess.

In the course of our discussion, Art shared with me his definition of success, particularly as it related to his cousin. "The success of a man is not measured by what heights he has risen to, but by what depths he has climbed from." Art Miller's cousin got things right with his Lord and Saviour. As a result of the spiritual cleansing in his life, God made him a totally new creation. His attitudes changed. His thought life changed. His perspective changed. His priorities changed. From the day of his new birth, God withheld no good thing from him. This did not mean that all his problems were gone. It did not mean overwhelming financial success. But it did mean that he could draw upon all the resources of heaven, for he was now a child of the King and a member of the great family of God. God wants the very best for His sons and daughters. Hudson Taylor said, "God always gives the very best to those who leave the choice to Him."

This chapter will deal with eight principles in a design for successful living. In many ways this will be a review of the entire book and will highlight the key areas essential to achieving the full potential God intends for your life.

Set and Maintain High Standards

"Only conduct yourselves in a manner worthy of the Gospel of Christ" (Philippians 1:27).

The Apostle Paul was very demanding of new believers. If the world was to be evangelized, it would be done by people who lived the life! Now that is surely a high goal, and high goals demand sacrifice if they are to be accomplished.

When Georgia's governor Jimmy Carter began to make plans to reside at 1600 Pennsylvania Avenue, he was attempting what many people considered the impossible. But Carter surrounded himself with a dedicated and loyal few who were willing to face all odds to reach a high goal.

During the snowy, blustery days of the New Hampshire primary, this small group kept their eyes on the big goal, but knew that a series of short-range goals had to be accomplished first. So they faced the formidable weather and went knocking on doors—all the doors they could find—and handed out a cost-conscious brochure which said, "Hi, I'm Jimmy Carter and I want to be your President."

Carter won that primary and kept on winning. By the time of the New York and Pennsylvania primaries, he was surrounded by thousands everywhere he went. He had gone from "Jimmy who?" to "Who doesn't know Jimmy?" in six months. It required dedication and diligence to not lose sight of the goal or slacken the standards necessary to achieve it.

Develop a Problem-Solving Attitude

"Do not fear, for I have redeemed you; I have called you by name; you are Mine! When you pass through the waters, I will be with you; and through the rivers, they shall not overflow you, when you walk through the fire, you will not be scorched, nor will the flame burn you. For I am the Lord your God, the Holy One of Israel, your Saviour; I have given Egypt as your ransom, Cush and Seba in your place" (Isaiah 43:1-3).

Although God has promised that the waters of life will not overflow us, He has also given us minds to evaluate the circumstances of each situation. We are not puppets being maneuvered in a master chess game. Quite the contrary. For God is anxious that we willfully declare our desire for fellowship with Him. In response He will give us the wisdom to reason and evaluate the problems and pressures of life. Job declared, "Man is born unto trouble, as the sparks fly upward" (Job 5:7, KJV). Trouble is a fact of life. Let's take a look at one practical plan to help us understand and solve everyday problems.

The problem-solving process begins by asking the Lord for a generous portion of His wisdom as it relates to the problem. Commit the problem to Him and ask Him to establish your thoughts and your thinking process so that the resolution will bring the most glory and honor to Him.

We all have problems to solve. If we reach facility in problem-solving, we can also learn to prevent many problems before they arise. But to do so requires hard work, for there is a wide range of problems that bring you face to face with challenge:

● New problems for which you lack decision guides.

● Problems experienced before, but still lacking sure decision guides.

● More familiar problems for which you have developed policies and guidelines.

● Frequently encountered problems for which you have standard decision rules.

The key thing to remember is that the problem-solving method is systematic. Even the most difficult and seemingly intangible problem can be solved. The intent is to replace ambiguity and the related anxiety with clear direction and concrete decision criteria.

Decision-making is the process by which alternatives are evaluated, selected, and committed to action. It is that part of the total problem-solving process that consciously and systematically deals with all of the relevant personal and situational information available to us.

The five steps of the scientific method are: get all the facts, sift out the important points, define the problem (root cause), formulate and evaluate alternative solutions, and make a decision (take action).

The value of being scientific about behavior is that we can have greater control over our lives. Persons who follow no systematic procedure for testing alternatives and drawing conclusions move haphazardly from one choice to another.

The problem-solving process is often frustrating. We can feel so overwhelmed by the data, that it seems we are going in circles rather than moving closer to our goals. However, people who utilize a scientific approach are able to identify objectively what is relevant, and then to integrate the data and select a course of action that will move them toward their goals. In effect, they are scientists of their own behavior.

Because the problem-solving process is influenced directly and indirectly by many factors, it cannot be divorced from the behavior of the problem-solver. There are at least six psychologically based tendencies that serve as barriers to effective problem-solving. These tendencies are:

● To evaluate rather than investigate, and become too involved emotionally.

● To equate new experiences with old. Often things that

look the same are quite different.

- To act in haste with readily available solutions. This can create more problems.
- To deal with problems at face value.
- To confuse symptoms and problems. This is to use the Band-Aid approach when surgery is needed.
- To overlook problems that seem unsolvable. This is a snare and a pitfall. Every problem is solvable and the problem will not go away simply by ignoring it. Unfortunately, if you begin to believe that some problems are unsolvable, you will be surprised how many of these you will have. Many of life's greatest opportunities come brilliantly disguised as problems.

Learn to Cope with Disappointment
"And Joshua said, 'Alas, O Lord God, why didst Thou ever bring this people over the Jordan, only to deliver us into the hand of the Amorites, to destroy us? If only we had been willing to dwell beyond the Jordan!'"(Joshua 7:7)

It seems hard to believe that the man who wrote these discouraged words is the person who said sometime later, "Choose for yourselves today whom you will serve ... as for me and my house, we will serve the Lord" (Joshua 24:15).

What are some of the main sources of disappointment and why?
- Ourselves—lack of achievement
            —lack of discipline
            —behavior to others
- Family—lack of encouragement
            —insensitive comments
- Friends—competitive behavior
            —"put-downs"
            —lack of follow-through on commitments

Disappointments result from expectations which were not met. The reasons for this are many. But regardless of the "why," disappointment is the initiating factor for depression.

What are some ways to overcome disappointments?

● Expect them, not cynically but realistically. We live in a world of imperfect people who will unintentionally disappoint us.

● Set realistic goals. Since expectations are the main source of disappointment, set goals which are attainable.

● Ask yourself these questions:

—"Why and how did it happen?"

—"How important was it really to me?"

—"Am I exaggerating the situation and feeling sorry for myself?"

—"Am I willing to forgive the person or group responsible for this disappointment?"

—"Have I ever disappointed others in the same way?"

—"What can I do to help the person or group who disappointed me, so that they don't do the same thing to others?"

Always remember this principle—"Failures are NEVER final! Praise the Lord!"

Strive for Self-Discipline

"But I do not consider my life of any account as dear to myself, in order that I may finish my course, and the ministry which I received from the Lord Jesus, to testify solemnly of the Gospel of the grace of God" (Acts 20:24).

Paul had many opportunities to get off track. He had been face to face with death and even that didn't budge him one inch off course. Why? He was determined to complete the ministry the Lord gave him. He never fell victim to saying or believing that it couldn't be done.

We are, by nature, very undisciplined. Without structure to our lives, we would spend our time merely surviving. It is not until we structure our time and energy with goals, and visualize ourselves accomplishing them, that we begin to truly enjoy life to the fullest. But that demands discipline.

The two major areas in which we need to discipline ourselves are: negative self-talk and the setting of priorities.

● Negative self-talk. Self-talk is the private conversation

we have with ourselves. It is the ultimate governing influence on our behavior. Remember, we do what we believe, not what we know. We believe what we say to ourselves. How do you overcome negative self-talk?

Meditate. Learn Scripture and hide it in your heart. Memorize and meditate upon the things of the Lord. Specifically dwell on the principles of thought found in Philippians 4:7-8. Here Paul is saying that if you want the peace of God which the world cannot comprehend, then you should think and dwell on things that are true, honest, just, pure, lovely, of good report, virtuous, and worthy of praise. In other words, you can protect your thought life by dwelling on the positive attitudes God has given to you.

Repeat positive affirmations. Thoughts imprint images on our minds. These thoughts cause us to behave in a way which conforms us to the image imprint. Therefore, the more positive the thought, the more positive the behavior. Say things like, "Wow! what a great family I belong to!" or "What a marvelous opportunity God has given me!"

Let me encourage you to never again say, "I can't." You can replace that statement with this one, "Up until now I have not been able to do it." "I can't" refers to the future. To say "I can't" is equivalent to admitting and confirming that you will never be able to do it. However, when you say, "Up until now" you are merely admitting to a fact of the past. But you are not confirming anything for the future.

Pursue personal challenge. A person who engages in negative self-talk very often is negative about other people. Therefore, in order to help yourself, will you take this challenge? Look at your watch, record the time and date, and then see how long you can go without saying something negative about anyone. You will discover that there is a direct correlation between negative self-talk and negative talk about others.

● Setting priorities. What are the priorities for life? This question has baffled mankind in every generation. We are all unique and must set our own goals and establish our own hierarchy of priorities. As a matter of fact, we are fulfilling our own priority systems every day.

Daily we make decisions as to what we are going to accomplish. Some people accomplish a great deal and others very little. Either way is a matter of choice, tempered with ability. While we do not have equal abilities, we all can choose to do our very best with what we have.

Most people accomplish little because they do not know how to get out from under the weight of all that has to be done. They cannot see the forest for the trees.

The first thing we should do every day is the thing we least want to do. If we were to follow that rule, we would accomplish a great deal. Instead, we tend to wrestle for so long with the "big" problem or the undesirable task that we finally throw up our hands and get very little done. If we get the bad job out of the way, we can face the day and its activities with new vigor and a real desire to get things done.

Each city of ancient Greece was known for something unique. Athens, for example, was the center of culture and learning, and Sparta was known for warriors who were tenaciously self-disciplined. Spartan soldiers were trained with extreme discipline and were often called on to endure great hardships.

In their training, they were taught an interesting and somewhat paradoxical principle. Should they be so unfortunate as to be surrounded by five or six enemy soldiers, they were to run away. Doesn't that sound a little odd for fierce warriors? Nevertheless, that was the rule. They were to run, not because they were afraid, but to employ the age-old strategy of divide and conquer.

They were in such great physical condition that when they ran away, the enemy troops began to drop off one by one. Every once in a while, a Spartan soldier would glance over his shoulder and see another enemy fall by the wayside, unable to keep the pace. Finally, he would look back and discover there was only one left. Then he would turn around and fight.

There are many lessons we can learn from this illustration. Problems must be reduced to a size we can handle—one at a time. As the Spartan faced the strongest foe first and then proceeded to face the others, so we can tackle the hardest job first.

It takes discipline to keep our priorities in line and our eyes fixed on a goal. But who said it was easy? Success never is!

Develop Communication Skills

"So then faith comes from hearing, and hearing by the word of Christ" (Romans 10:17).

We live in a most peculiar culture where we are influenced to buy everything—from bubble gum to expensive automobiles —simply because some celebrity endorses the product. When you think about it—what do most of these people know about shaving cream or coffee or toothpaste or aspirins? But we believe this nonsense because we ridiculously transfer the public image of the celebrities to the products they are endorsing, and are mystically reassured.

This same transfer relationship happens with one who articulately communicates. If an orator has learned the techniques of voice control, timing, and content, he will deliver a great speech. If he has learned the art of persuasive communication and is therefore believable, we tend to be more susceptible to his message. Not only are we vulnerable, but we tend to ascribe to the speaker abilities he doesn't have. We simply cannot imagine a person that fluent and dynamic not being able to answer all our problems.

We tend to exaggerate the abilities of a persuasive speaker and give him more areas of responsibility. This is called *leadership emergence.* It is generally recognized that the one who speaks with authority and confidence controls the group. Therefore, the one who fits this mold is often given more opportunities, more possibilities for growth, more leadership roles. As a result, he gains more confidence.

Since this is true, we should examine the communication

process in an effort to maximize our skills. For we can be sure that Satan is not anxious for God's children to communicate effectively.

● A general model of communication. Each day as we communicate with other people, we use different modes of speaking, listening, writing, reading, and nonverbal communication. Whatever the medium, there are four elements basic to all communication:

      —A person to originate a thought or idea
      —The idea itself, as it is expressed
      —A medium or channel for expressing the idea
      —Someone to receive and interpret the idea

This communication process can be summarized by examining the following model:

Steps:

—Ideation by the sender. This is the intended content of the message the sender wants to transmit. The sender has ideas, intentions, information, and a purpose for communicating.

—Encoding the message. The ideas are organized in a suitable context for the transmission medium in order that the ideas and purposes can be expressed as a message.

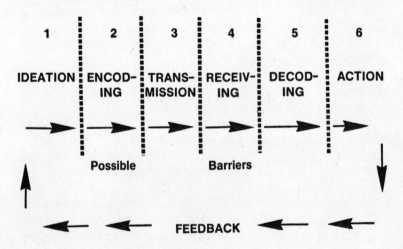

—Transmission of the message as encoded through the selected medium.

—Receiving the intended message. Here the receiver enters the process by tuning in to receive the message.

—Decoding the receiver. The message must be decoded in terms of relevance to the receiver.

—Action by the receiver. In this step the receiver acts or responds by filing the information, asking for more information, or taking other action.

—Feedback to the sender. Communication has taken place only when there is some form of acknowledgment given to the sender that the message was received.

● Effective personal communication. Improving one's communication with others requires commitment to such a process. This process requires a climate that is trusting and supportive in order that the feedback, so essential to improving our ability to communicate, can be given and received in a way that encourages listening and acceptance, rather than increased defensiveness.

Consider the following personal communication goals:

—An awareness that I am a person with feelings and that I can live with the fact that my feelings influence me and my communication.

—A tolerance of other people's feelings and an awareness that their feelings, which may be different than mine, affect their sending and receiving of communications.

—The intention as sender to build feelings of security in the receiver.

—The intention, as receiver, to listen from the sender's point of view rather than evaluate the communication from my own.

—The willingness to take more than half the responsibility for the effectiveness of communication, whether as sender or receiver.

—The conscious effort to build feedback into all communications.

—The ability to resist acting on or reacting to my

assumptions about another person's reasons behind a particular communication.

—A recognition that communications are at best imperfect, and the avoidance of undue cynicism resulting from difficulties or failures to communicate.

Develop Rapport with Others

"And when he had said these things, he knelt down and prayed with them all. And they began to weep aloud and embraced Paul, and repeatedly kissed him, grieving especially over the word which he had spoken, that they should see his face no more. And they were accompanying him to the ship" (Acts 20:36-38).

The broad meaning of *rapport* is to be in agreement or in harmony with others. This requires a willingness to invest ourselves in others, to ascertain what their needs are, and to try to meet them faithfully.

As you review these questions, ask the Lord to reveal your blind spots to you:

- Have you qualified for the role of the peacemaker?
- Are you entrusted with the handling of difficult and delicate situations?
- Do you find it easy to make and keep friends?
- Are you at ease in the presence of your supervisors or strangers?
- Are you really interested in people?
- Do you nurse resentments, or do you readily forgive injuries done to you?
- Do you use people or cultivate people?
- Do other people's failures annoy you or challenge you?
- Do you criticize or encourage people?
- Do you shun the problem person or seek him out?

Develop a Helping Attitude

Recently I was at supper with a man who produces training films. He travels the nation securing the talent necessary to make his movies. Some time ago, he came across an idea for a movie while watching an actor on one of the sets. The successful actor/businessman spent a great deal of time giving of himself to others. He did anything that needed to be done and helped anyone who needed help, even in little things.

Later this producer made a movie called *The Go-Giver*. We often hear the expression "go-getter." But a "go-giver" is one who is not afraid to give because he knows that getting is directly proportional to giving.

One of God's laws is, "Give, and it will be given to you" (Luke 6:38). The principle is to give according to your need. In other words, whatever you need, you give. Sound like a paradox? It is!

Our family was enjoying a beautiful day at New Smyrna Beach on the Atlantic side of Florida. Our oldest son, Paul, was a senior in high school at the time and was struggling with finding direction for his life. In the middle of a Frisbee game he asked me, "Dad, what does it mean, 'Give, and it shall be given unto you'?"

Donna and I both thought that this was an excellent opportunity to share this principle with the children. We called them all together on the shelter of the sand dunes and set about to answer Paul's sensitive question. I mounded a pile of white sand. Making a clenched fist I asked Paul if he would agree that this would symbolize taking. He agreed. Then opening my hand with the palm upright I asked if he would agree that this symbolized giving. He agreed. I then asked him to make a fist and then reach into the pile of sand and take as much as he could get. He did and held his big clenched fist up high with the sand pouring out every gap it could find. "How much have you got?" I asked. "Nothing." "Now reach your open hand into that pile of sand and give as much as you can." With the open palm, Paul held a pile of sand in his hand.

Many years ago, a wealthy family from England were vacationing in the Highlands of Scotland. One day the family was picnicking by a fast-flowing mountain river. In the course of their activity they did not realize that their young son had wandered off. Nor did they hear his cries for help as he was carried down river. But a young shepherd boy who was tending his sheep heard and raced down the slopes, dove into the river, and saved the little boy's life.

The shepherd boy went back to his sheep and the other boy back to his parents who were overcome with joy. They wanted to find the shepherd boy who had been so brave and looked for three days to locate his little thatched cottage. For several hours they tried to persuade the boy's mom and dad to take a reward. Finally, the parents agreed to accept the gift of education for the young boy.

The years passed and the shepherd boy finished high school and went on to college and medical school. His name was Alexander Fleming, the discoverer of penicillin who was later knighted for his contribution to mankind. The boy who was willing to risk his life to save another was given the great blessing of discovering a substance which would save the lives of countless millions.

By the way, the little boy whose life he saved was Winston Churchill. As an adult, Churchill was the second person ever to receive a shot of penicillin and it saved his life. Sir Alexander Fleming was directly responsible twice for saving Winston Churchill's life.

No Compromise

"But I do not consider my life of any account as dear to myself, in order that I may finish my course, and the ministry which I received from the Lord Jesus, to testify solemnly of the Gospel of the grace of God" (Acts 20:24).

Churchill's final speech was given to a graduating class of the War Academy. The hall was filled to capacity. Churchill was introduced and the crowd waited expectantly as the greatest orator of modern times walked feebly to the podium. He took a long, solemn stare across the hall and raised his hand to his eyes to scan every riveted face. Then he said these words, "Never give up, never give up, never give up!"

In Isaiah 50:7 we read the words of the coming Messiah: "I have set My face like flint, and I know that I shall not be ashamed."

You too can set your face like a flint. You can finish what you have started. Do not compromise on what God has shown you for your life. Remember, "No good thing does He withhold from them that walk uprightly."

"Of all the sad words of tongue or pen,
the saddest of all are—it could have been."
                                        John Greenleaf Whittier

Victor Books for the Inner You

Do You Hear What You're Thinking?
by Jerry Schmidt
The Bible says that as a person "thinks within himself, so is he." Learn how to control the thoughts that control your actions.

Healing for Damaged Emotions by David Seamands
Satan uses many emotional problems to keep Christians from reaching spiritual maturity. Learn how to heal these problems with God's help.

Overcoming Stress by Jan Markell with Jane Winn
Today's Christians are often exposed to greater stresses than non-Christians. Learn how to overcome stress before it overcomes you.

The Power Delusion by Anthony Campolo, Jr.
Human beings hunger for power, yet Christ's call is to servanthood and humility. Can power and humility co-exist? What should the Christian's attitude be toward power?

The Success Fantasy by Anthony Campolo, Jr.
This book offers a penetrating analysis of the contemporary idolatry of success. Learn how to stop living on substitutes and become successful in God's eyes.

The Time of Your Life by Mark Porter
Jesus finished His earthly work without "scurry syndrome." His example and biblical principles provide time-management ideas that can help you accomplish more.